Lost & Found
Spirituality for a Changing World

To John

with prayers &
blessings

Michael

Photos
Front Cover – The Maze at Leeds Castle,
kind permission of Leeds Castle Foundation.
Back Cover – www.photo-digital.co.uk

Editor's Note
For ease of reading, I have only included the Chapter numbers for scripture references within the text, too much reference detail can distract from the reading.

ISBN 978-0-9548388-8-1
© Don Bosco Publications 2007
Thornleigh House
Sharples Park
BOLTON BL1 6PQ
Email michael@salesians.org.uk
www.don-bosco-publications.co.uk

CONTENTS

Chapter 1 — Discovering who we are in God

There is only one problem on which all my existence, my peace and happiness depend: to discover myself in discovering God. If I find Him I will find myself and if I find my true self I will find Him.[1]

God's love for us is fundamental for our lives, and it raises important questions about who God is and who we are.[2]

Our times are sombre, yet full of hope. What is beyond dispute is that they are times of rapid and unsettling change. It seems that we are living uneasily between the poles of fear and love. The fearful voices often seem to be in the ascendancy creating a climate of deep anxiety and mistrust. This strikes a chord with many who seem to have lost their bearings, who don't know where they are going. We are on a journey and we can't find our way home. Even the very means of transport have become centres of terror. The recent alleged plot to blow up several transatlantic jets resulted in long and chaotic queues of travellers and families trying to get away on holiday. What should be a time of relaxation and rest has been turned into a potential nightmare: the tighter the security, the greater the anxiety. Even when plots are foiled, the terrorists appear to win. Walking along a street recently, I overheard a conversation between a woman and her grandson. He was due to fly off on holiday with his parents and family. They were discussing the terrorist threat to air travel; the boy concluded stoically that there was nothing you could do: when your number is up, that is it. I estimated that the boy was little more than nine or ten years old.

The growth in fear created by terrorism threatens much of our western world. It undermines us at a time when other profound changes have unsettled us. Previously, we have looked to our leaders to provide hope and vision in a time of change. The changes we are undergoing now are so fundamental that no one seems to know what to do. We seem lost. Very few politicians are able to articulate a compelling vision of the future. The great hope of the Enlightenment was that education and science rather than religion would be sufficient to liberate humanity. This hope collapsed with the death of over 100 million people in the wars of the twentieth century. The twenty-first century has begun

---

1 Thomas Merton *New Seeds of Contemplation* (New Directions 1972) p 36

2 Benedict XVI *Deus Caritas Est* (CTS 2006) p 5

with similar violence and conflict. Education now, with some brave exceptions, seems to be trapped in a predominantly utilitarian straightjacket. The search for knowledge has been hijacked by the search for employment. Work is an important and necessary part of life; but on its own, it doesn't lead us into the bigger picture. The Church, too, has also lost the confidence of society and is often perceived as being on the side of reaction and fear. Since it is unsure what to say to the world, it seems to have turned inward by concentrating on micro-management in areas such as liturgical language. Repeated surveys document peoples' fears of crime and violence, of drug addiction, the collapse of family values, and the increase in teenage pregnancies, of abortions; fears surrounding increasing immigration and fears about the fate of the planet. We are no longer a confident civilisation: the future is uncertain.

Our sense of loss and confusion is so profound that I think that what is happening to us can only be described as a spiritual crisis. In losing our sense of direction and purpose, we are forced to face the deepest human questions. What does it mean to be human today? In a world of rapid globalisation, how can we create a society that places the human being at the centre, rather than money and greed? How do we care for our planet, as we demand more and more of its resources? How do we respond to the unprecedented mass-migration of peoples that is happening today? While these questions touch on our public and civic life, they also touch upon our individual souls.

Throughout history, idealistic people have struggled to reform and renew society. Great revolutions have taken place, as enlightened people have fought for, and often died on behalf of the poor and the excluded. Most of these great revolutions, such as the French Revolution or the Communist Revolution, have started out on the left, with the aim of improving the lot of the disadvantaged. Yet they all seem to have ended up on the right, with new elite in power and a different set of oppressors and oppressed. It is one thing to attempt to change society; it is a much more challenging task to change ourselves. Politics, sociology, education and psychology cannot address this core problem. It has to engage the soul; it is a spiritual challenge. I would suggest that our sense of loss and alienation today is simply manifesting a crisis of spirituality: a crisis which cannot be resolved by increasing the *membership* of our churches. As long as the Church seeks simply to increase its members, it will not address the true nature of the crisis. In recent years, I have travelled to many parts of the world and preached retreats to religious orders of men and women and to lay people: in religious circles the question I have been asked more than any other is: *Are you getting more vocations?* I think that there is a more fundamental question to be asked and the answer has implications both for the renewal of our personal lives and the life of our societies. As always in healthy spirituality, the personal and the political come together.

I am convinced that the key issue today is *transformation*. Transformation involves more than social reform; it calls for change at the deepest level of our souls. This is the classic spiritual journey. It is the only way home. Only transformation will help us to address the core issues that our politics, whether conservative or liberal, and our individual lives, are failing to address. We cannot take others into any kind of *Promised Land* unless we ourselves have made some kind of spiritual journey. Transformation is necessary because it teaches us that we human beings have to learn how to deal with the parts of life that we cannot fix, with its hurts, its conflicts, its disappointments, its injustices. In a word, we have to learn how to deal with evil, with pain and with suffering. Unless we can find a way to deal with these experiences on life's journey, and let them transform us, we will have nothing to offer in the second half of life. We will have become bitter, disillusioned and cynical, as many are today. We all begin with plenty of hope and idealism in the first half of life. Then we meet some experience of pain and suffering, of setback, something that we cannot fix. If we do not know how to let this kind of experience teach us, then we can get very angry and bitter, and look for someone else to blame. There are many bitter and angry people today.

In a constantly changing and uncertain world like ours, this pain has become very acute. We live in an age of anxiety and none of us likes anxiety. We look for someone else, or some other group, or some other nation or religion to blame. Any pain, which is not transformed, is simply transmitted and projected onto someone else. This is not *healthy spirituality;* it is *junk spirituality*. This can be equally true of members of Churches, as well as those who have no allegiance. It is a core human question: spirituality exists to teach us what it means to be human. What we learn from healthy spirituality is that there is a deep pre-existing union that exists in all of us, irrespective of nation, creed or colour. It is what makes us most human. We are all carriers of the image of God. This is foundational. Our very being is blessed and marked with grace.

This union is a gift. It cannot be earned or bought and, in that sense, it contradicts the deepest tenet of the capitalist system, which controls most of our world and infiltrates our souls. What this gift of union demands of us is some kind of *surrender*. Here also it radically undercuts our obsession today with controlling and fixing. This vision of union and communion, once understood and surrendered to, leads us to a much bigger and more spacious place than the private world of the individual. It leads us from trying to force everyone else into our particular viewpoint or culture and takes us to a place where all people can feel at home. It means that we have been found at the deepest level of our being and our souls. This is the meaning of what religious language calls *salvation*. It takes us out of the world of fear and anxiety, and places us securely in a world of love. It means that even though we feel lost we have all been found. The issue is always one of seeing rightly, of becoming aware of who we really are. This kind of awareness has to be a personal experience; nobody else can have it for us. Everybody needs some kind of *absolute* to surrender to; if we can't bring ourselves to surrender to God, then we will be lost on the wheel of life, like a mouse in a cage: plenty of activity but not much wisdom.

The culture that formerly handed on faith to the next generation has largely gone, despite the heroic work of many of our teachers, which is why personal experience is so crucial. The landscape of today has shifted and changed beyond recognition. As Michael Paul Gallagher explains:

> **Throughout most of human history, cultures have been rooted in religious consciousness; a central crisis of culture today comes from the split between culture and religion over the last two centuries or so.**[3]

That religious culture no longer exists; it has resulted, in Christian circles, in a consequent shift from the experience of authority to the authority of experience. This development is offering believers the opportunity to ask deeper spiritual questions. Perhaps we have been guilty of reducing religion to a predominantly *moral matter*, a question of obeying laws. In contrast, we see Jesus in the gospels telling us who we are and who God is, for us. He declared that our identity cannot be created by moral behaviour; it is, in fact, wholly given. This gift goes beyond anything we could ever deserve. Jesus leads us into a new realm of grace and unconditional love, in which each of us is a beloved son or daughter, and God is our Father. While the Pharisees and Scribes had reduced religion to a matter of law and observance, a system based on personal worthiness; Jesus moves us to a different level. He moves us into a bigger picture, which He calls *The Kingdom of God.* The problem with law-based religion is that it keeps the ego firmly in place. We can all assess and monitor our behaviour, and tick off our good deeds. The ego loves such a programme, because it allows us to feel good about ourselves. While this false self remains in control, no transformation is possible.

From a position of moral superiority, it is so easy to judge and condemn others. It is this judgemental attitude that seems to turn so many people off religion today. All you have to do is to identify the evil over there, in someone

---

3 Michael Paul Gallagher *Clashing Symbols* (Darton Longman &Todd 1997) p 23

else, or some other group, and then fight it. In its extreme form, this is the spirituality of the terrorist; so convinced of moral righteousness, that others who disagree can be killed; in the name of God. All of us manifest something of this judgemental mentality when we compare others less favourably with ourselves.

Jesus begins his public ministry by calling for repentance. That word has largely lost its meaning for us today. Using a Greek word, Jesus asked for *metanoia*, or *meta nous*, calling for a complete change of mind, a different kind of thinking. The old way of thinking will always block transformation. Even religion can be one of the most effective ways of doing this, when it tries to change others, to punish sinners, to expel those who fail. Unless there is some personal ownership of my own need to change then transformation will not happen, my heart will remain untouched. For this to occur I must be led into the new realm of grace that Jesus proclaims. This is a new understanding of the God who loves me deeply and accepts me at the very core of my being. The Bible uses the expression *Do not be afraid*, 365 times.

Our contemporary culture says that there are no overall patterns of meaning that make sense today; consequently each individual must create his or her own significance. This puts an intolerable burden on the individual, it probably accounts for so much of our current unhappiness and stress levels. Sociological and psychological surveys remind us that, despite increasing levels of affluence in the western world, our culture is not a happy one. We have lost something essential to our humanity. We feel lost and we don't know who we are. The more we buy and consume, the less satisfied we feel. Zygmunt Bauman accurately describes contemporary culture as *skating on thin ice*. Thus, we are compelled, for safety reasons, simply to keep on moving. In rejecting the spiritual claim of eternal life, we try to find eternity now, in an endless cycle of consumption. Goods are created with built-in obsolescence, leaving us in a constant state of anxiety to acquire the latest and most up-to-date model. Our upwardly-mobile men and women of today are told by the advertising industry that they can have it all, but only at the cost of endless running and consuming. Bauman calls this *liquid life* and it feeds on self-dissatisfaction.[4] A recent movie called *Crank*, a rather mindless violent thriller, tells the story of a man injected with a deadly poison by his enemy. As long as his adrenaline level remains suitably high, he will survive; once it drops, he will die: hence the frenetic energy level of the plot. It is an ironic comment on our times.

---

4 Zygmunt Bauman *Liquid Life* (Polity Press Cambridge 2006)

Spirituality moves us to a different place. It invites us to make the journey within, to discover *the pearl of great price*. It gives us an identity transplant. It reveals the staggering fact that God lives within us, in our hearts, in our souls. We are led into the paradox of wisdom, which tells us that God dwells within us and at the same time is utterly beyond. This is not something the rational mind can comprehend. It leads us beyond the calculating mind of left-brain logic and analysis, to the more feminine right brain that can embrace paradox and mystery. This yearning for mystery and beauty is at the heart of the spiritual journey today. I am suggesting the paradox, that in our spiritual journey we are both *lost and found*, at the same time. We are *lost* to the extent that we forget who we are. We are *found* when we remember that God is closer to us than we are to ourselves. This is the paradox of mystery and miracle that frames our lives.

It takes time to allow this mystery to transform us. In this life, we never get it all together. In the gospels, Jesus is clearly aware that it takes time to get this good news across to people. There is clearly some staging in his teaching. He refers to his need to leave us, so that the Holy Spirit can continue to teach us:[5]

> **The Friend, the Holy Spirit, whom the Father will send at my request, will make everything plain to you. He will remind you of all the things I have told you.** *John 14*

When we learn to live with paradox and mystery, then we can rest in the fact that we don't know everything; that we don't always understand; that there are things that we cannot fix, because we can acknowledge our own weakness and imperfection, rather than spend our energy trying to fix the weaknesses of others. This calls for great humility and compassion. Jesus told the parable of the wise and foolish virgins. We tend to read that in an either/or mode, because that is the normal way of thinking of the calculative mind. As a wisdom teacher, Jesus leads us into the more contemplative mind that can hold both together. This parable may well be teaching us that sometimes we can show wisdom but at other times, we may act foolishly. We have to learn to own both these realities and that is how transformation happens: not by being perfect, but by having the humility to learn from our weaknesses, which may have more to teach us than our strengths.

An essential element of true spirituality is that it always leads us to a place of honesty and humility. This is the new humanity that Jesus is trying to create: a humanity that can, on the one hand, admit its wounds and weaknesses, and

---

5 Peterson translation

on the other celebrate and give thanks for the presence of the God within. Not many of us want to live with the tension of being both lost and found, at the same time. Some present us with Christianity as a religion of the *lost*; we are all sinners and nothing will ever change. Others present us with Christianity as a religion of the *found*; everything is fine. Jesus asks us to carry the mystery of the cross, our weakness and failure, and rejoice in the glory of the resurrection - God's life, living in us. To help us reach this level of spiritual maturity, we don't find Jesus asking us to worship him in the gospels. In a sense that can be quite easy, but he frequently asks his disciples to follow him, which is much more difficult, because the path he led them on was the journey of descent into suffering and death. This is why we find transformation difficult. Something in me has to die, my egocentric self. The ego is very subtle and will find all kinds of ways to fight this, as we will see in a later chapter.

I want to suggest that many of the profound changes happening today should not be the cause of anxiety and fear. I think that much of what is occurring is, in fact, the work of the Holy Spirit. Rather than retreat into pessimism and cynicism, we need to reach out to embrace the new world that is being created before our eyes. This is not naïve optimism, since changes as deep as we are experiencing today cannot be brought about painlessly; but it is a call for hope. What we need is what Jesus so often asked for: faith and trust. Unfortunately, we may have reduced faith to believing in doctrines and dogma. Faith is primarily a profound attitude of trust and surrender to the mystery of life. It shifts the emphasis from the individual to the bigger picture, to God's presence in the world, in the kingdom. It calls for surrender despite much ambiguity and even doubt, rather than the easy certainty of catechism answers.

The great biblical figures were all led into this kind of faith and they struggled to bring a reluctant people along with them. They were taken out of the familiar, to face new challenges and discover God in new places and situations. Abraham is rightly called the father of this kind of faith, as he was asked to abandon his familiar world and journey into a new and strange land. When Moses led the people out of slavery in Egypt, we might expect Yahweh to give them an easy route to the Promised Land, but, in fact, God led them into a long and difficult journey:

> **When Pharaoh let the people go, God did not lead them by way of the land of the Philistines, although that was nearer ... So God led the people by the roundabout way of the wilderness towards the Red Sea.** *Exodus 13*

In the Bible God is constantly moving the people away from their comfort zone. Moses was aware of this pattern when he reminded the people:

> **The Lord God spoke to us at Horeb saying, You have stayed long enough at this mountain. Resume your journey.** *Deuteronomy 1*

In the New Testament, Jesus is frequently described as being on a journey, not in the frenetic sense of contemporary culture, but as an attempt to lead his followers into a new experience of God. The Judaism of Jesus' time was built on the great distinction between the worthy and the unworthy, the pure and the impure, the lost and the found. This was dramatically expressed in the various courtyards of the temple in Jerusalem. In the centre was the Holy of Holies, entered by the high priest once a year; next the courtyard of the priests and the Levites, then the courtyard of the Jewish males. Beyond that was the courtyard of Jewish women and for much of the year these women were judged too unclean to enter because of menstruation or childbirth. Next, was the area for the sick, the handicapped and the sinners, beyond that, and denied any entrance at all, were the lepers, the great outsiders of Jewish society.

Jesus goes out of his way to undermine this whole system of worthiness, by revealing to the excluded that they were indeed sons and daughters of God. All have access to God: the lost have been truly found. Rene Girard points out that all religions begin by making these false distinctions. Jesus, on the other hand, comes to reveal that Yahweh, his father, is the father of all. There are no exclusions. Everything and everyone belongs in the kingdom of radical grace. All share a common identity, a free gift, the unconditional love of God. In the letter to the Ephesians, the author sums up the mission - the plan of God, revealed in the Incarnation - as God reconciling *all things in heaven and on earth.*

The part of Merseyside where I live has recently acquired a recycling centre. I often feel that God is the great recycler. He takes every aspect of our lives and brings new life from it, and especially the bits that we feel embarrassed about. As a young religious, I was formed in the spirituality of perfection. Increasingly I see that the only spirituality that can lead us to adult faith these days is the spirituality of imperfection.

Here I can hold all the opposites together: good and bad, light and dark, strengths and weaknesses. In this space, I encounter the mercy and compassion of God and I discover that *when I am lost I am also found.* This is good news. In fact, it seems to be part of the pattern that we need to be lost, in order to find the extraordinary forgiveness and mercy of God. So being on a journey, when I am not sure where I am going, is not so fearful after all. God is always there to be found in the unexpected, in surprising places and in unlikely people. When Yahweh led the Hebrew people away from their comfort zones into new journeys, he was trying to form a people who would be open to His presence.

We are all relational beings, but the gift of becoming present is not easily acquired, especially in our frenetic age of constant activity. We have to find the balance between movement and stillness otherwise, we will be overwhelmed. Our liquid culture today does not lend itself easily to this. Time has to be set aside for the journey within. Only then can we learn the difficult art of being present to the God within and the God without. This involves learning not only to be present to others, especially to the poor and to the outsiders, but also learning to be present to the God who is found in the centre of my being, the God who gives me my true identity, my true self.

Chapter 2 — The Problem of the False Self

The core of our being is drawn like a stone to the quiet depths of each moment where God waits for us with eternal longing. But to those depths the false self will not let us travel.[6]

Our identity is rooted in the heart of God. We are created for union and intimacy with God. If this is the case, then we need to ask, *Why it is that many people live their lives with little awareness of this fact?* This includes many religious believers. Many church-going people understand religion as a series of duties, which need to be carried out, things that we have to do for God. It includes being a member of a Christian community and saying prayers. Clearly, these are all good things, but they are secondary rather than primary. Christianity is not primarily a moral code or a set of beliefs; it is a relationship that summons us to a face-to-face encounter with God. This is the reality of transformation, and is always the work of God. Our task is to surrender to the activity of God and that always involves a certain amount of dying. We can ask, *Why is this? What is it, that has to die?* Put simply it is the false self, but this needs some clarification and explanation.

In contemporary spirituality, Thomas Merton rescued the language of the false self and the true self to describe the spiritual conflict, which all of us experience. Other writers such as Basil Pennington, Richard Rohr, and Robert Muholland Jnr have explored this foundational struggle in our lives. All of them, however, are only recovering crucial insights set out by the apostle Paul. Perhaps one of the reasons why Paul's understanding fell into disuse is because of the language he uses. For Paul, the spiritual struggle is between the *flesh* and the *spirit.*

As soon as we hear the word *flesh* we immediately equate it with the body, and we very quickly get lost in the misleading idea that Paul is attacking and dismissing the body. This is a serious distortion of what Paul is talking about when he is contrasting *flesh* and *spirit.* When he uses the word *flesh,* he is speaking of illusion and falsehood, of what is going to die and disappear. Sadly, many of us Christians are, in fact, Platonists. Plato was a dualist who contrasted *body* with *spirit. Body* was bad and had to be denied, *spirit* on the other hand was good. In fact, there can be much falsehood in the realm of *spirit* just as there can be goodness in the *body.* So, Paul contrasts *flesh* and *spirit,* not *body* and *spirit.*

---

6 James Finley *Merton's Palace of Nowhere* (Ave Maria Press, Indiana 1978,1999) p 26

A good insight into how Paul understood flesh is found in his letter to the Galatians.[7]

> **Live freely, animated and motivated by God's Spirit. Then you won't feed the compulsions of selfishness. For there is a root of sinful self-interest in us that it is at odds with a free spirit, just as the free spirit is incompatible with selfishness. These two ways of life are antithetical, so that you cannot live at times one way and at times another way according to how you feel on any given day.** *Galatians 5*

Phrases such as *compulsions of selfishness* and *sinful self-interest* capture what Paul means by *living in the flesh*. The false self is the independent *I*, the small self, the autonomous, separate-existent self that we think we are. It is the lost self, the small self, in contrast with the true self, which we shall explore more fully in the next chapter. The true self is the realm of shared consciousness, the self which is fundamentally related to and connected to the bigger picture, the God-Self. What Paul is trying to get across is that once you understand the realm of the spirit, the little independent self just fades away. This is why he uses vivid expressions such as:

> **I live, no longer I, but Christ lives in me. Our life is hidden with Christ in God.** *Colossians 3*

The word *hidden* is especially important because we are dealing with something in the realm of mystery, something that is beyond our control and even our understanding.

The false or small self can be defined as who you think you are, before transformation. The true self is who you know you are after transformation. It is not a question of becoming more church-going, or more pious, or more religious. As we shall see, that can sometimes prevent the true self from emerging. At the heart of this issue is the great spiritual fact that something has to die if we are to move from our false self. This is crucial to our understanding; otherwise we fight the wrong spiritual battle. For many, this wrong battle is centred on the body, which we think has to be suppressed. Too many Christians feel a deep shame about their bodies. This is not what Paul is addressing. For him the real battle is between the false and the true self. Paul doesn't oppose the flesh with *law*, but with *spirit*. Mere observance of the law gets me trapped into performance-principle religion, the mistaken idea that I have to do good

---

7 Peterson Translation

deeds in order to win God's favour. This is *ladder theology* and it is strongly rejected by Paul. Ladder theology suggests that we have to struggle to get to God and it tends to shape the spiritual life of most Christians, including priests and religious. For Paul, the opposite is true: it is God who struggles to get to us. Just think about that!

The false self is not really bad; it is just not the whole picture. It is always needy. It is rooted in the fact that none of us had perfect parents, or grew up in a perfect world. At times, our parents will have loved us unconditionally; at other times, our parents started to introduce conditions: *if you behave properly, if you put your toys away, if you eat your vegetables, if you work hard at school, then Mum and Dad will love you.*

In the normal run of family life, this has to happen; but the message we take on board is that we are not lovable as ourselves, but only because of what we do. It is precisely because of this wounding that the false self is created. We have to find some ways to protect ourselves from rejection and hurt. So we look to win our parents' approval, and the approval of others. Our false self is therefore created as a protective shell. It is made up of what I have, what I do, how I look, and what others think of me.

The false self needs constant affirmation because it doesn't know who it is. It has lost its true identity. It is not at home. The Bible begins with Adam and Eve being loved unconditionally in the Garden of Eden. When they break their link with God they choose the path of independence, they now have to create their own identity. Instead of living God-centred lives they are now on the path of self-centred lives. They have left the place of union with God, the place of unitive consciousness, and now live in a world of split consciousness. The temptation is brilliantly described when Adam and Eve are told that if they eat the forbidden fruit they will be just like God. That is the essence of the false self: to take over God's role in our lives, to cut ourselves off from God, to deny our true identity. God created us in *His own image* and the false self sets out to create God in *our* image. The whole of the Bible has been written outside the Garden and is seeking a way back. We are lost and we need to be found.

As a means of survival outside the Garden we have to constantly protect, defend and expand the false self. The world of the false self is based on fear as opposed to love. Our culture feeds the false self with the equally false promises of consumerism with its everyday world of retail therapy, *must have* items and the ever changing demands of fashion. I read an article in a Sunday newspaper the other day suggesting that iPods might be on the way out: since there were so many of them, they were no longer *cool*. The false self has to keep feeding these compulsions. We see a similar pattern in the current cult of celebrities, who themselves are divided into A B C and even D lists by the tabloid press. If I don't know who I am then one solution is to attach my insignificant self onto somebody else, someone famous. The false self leaves many people today trapped by low self-esteem. In such a condition it is all too easy to find one's significance in a cult of celebrity. Clever television producers have latched on to the insight that it can confer instant celebrity to the favoured few who participate in programmes such as The *X-Factor* and *Big Brother*, that offer instant fame and celebrity. The wider public can all share in this ritual by means of phone-ins and text messages. For many, fame has become a substitute religion, the religion of the false self.

Our problem is blindness. We have to let go of our illusions. True spirituality is always about learning to see. The great spiritual challenge is to discover what is real, the truth of things. The egocentric agenda of the false self prevents us from seeing the great truth, the bigger picture. This truth is often too much for our tiny controlling egos. True spirituality will always bring us back to the Garden. Perhaps the greatest loss today is that there are many who have lost their awareness that there is a Garden to return to. This is the great burden of secularism. For such people religious experience is forbidden territory, a forgotten memory. Great religion will always lead to a parting of the veil, reminding us of our primary experience of being known and loved at the deepest core of our being. Without this experience our lives are lived in the grip of all kinds of fears and anxieties and our largely secular culture continues to feed these fears and anxieties, by providing short-term fixes. There is always the latest movie to see, the new CD to buy and so on. These things are not bad but they keep us fixated at the surface level.

We either live our lives in the *fear worldview* or the *love worldview*. The fear worldview is what John's Gospel warns us about when he uses the word *world*. This is not the created world, which is good. Although, at times, Christians have often lived as if the world was the great enemy. John makes it clear that God does not condemn the world, since he sent his beloved son into the world, to bring us all into the mystery of forgiveness and mercy, what we call salvation. The negative sense of *world* for John is the system that props up the false self and prevents us from discovering our real and true identity. It sets me up against others who are perceived as threats to my reputation or fulfilment of my happiness. It is constantly judging and comparing others unfavourably. Basil Pennington describes it accurately as a fearful existence in which we are always living under the threat and anxiety that someone else will take from me what I have worked hard to acquire.

And it is a lonely place. We must never let others get too close. They might just discover what we so fearfully

know: that down beneath all that we have and all that we do is that little one who is all need and is ever trying to win the approbation of others in the hope that it might ultimately assure us that we are worth something.[8]

Some manage to hide their deepest fears and insecurities but others experience different forms of stress, depression and addiction. Because we do not really know who we are; we have no real means of learning from and being transformed by life's inevitable pain and suffering. Since we cannot deal with it, we find someone else to blame and to make the scapegoat. This is true both at the personal and·the political level. Our world today is beset by violent conflicts and wars, causing untold suffering. The great spiritual message we need to learn is that if we do not transform our pain we will transmit it. This is the great challenge of transformation.

If we want to test the authenticity of religion and spirituality, it always comes down to how we deal with the inevitable pain and conflicts of human existence. The false self doesn't know how to deal with pain as can be seen from the deep levels of anger in our world today. We have even invented a new phrase, *Road Rage*. The false self cannot deal with threats to its own agenda. Nothing must get in the way of the egocentric person. This anger may be manifested towards a particular person or group, or it simmers, as an underlying resentment, that can explode into an angry outburst that seems quite out of proportion to the incident that triggered it. This anger is supported by the culture of blame in which we live. We have to find someone else to blame or to sue for any negative thing that happens. Accidents are no longer allowed; it has to be somebody's fault. This has spawned a victim culture. Every problem I have is someone else's fault.

The language of responsibility has been overwhelmed by the language of individual rights. My private ego is no longer responsible for its actions. Our Christian tradition used to defend the doctrine of free will but this has almost disappeared from modern consciousness and we can all happily play the victim. Listen to radio and TV talk shows and you will hear the constant refrain: *I have been hurt, I have my rights, how do I get compensation?* There may well be genuine cases, but not even the most generous financial compensation can give me the true sense and value of my own dignity, which is a *gift* of God.

Healthy spirituality meets this head on when it teaches us that our wounds have to become our teachers. No court of law can ever do this. This is not a new problem, although it has almost taken over our culture today. It clearly

---

8 Basil Pennington *True Self False Self* (Crossroad Publishing Co New York 2000) p 35

existed in Paul's time as he takes the Corinthians to task for seeking to solve their differences and conflicts in secular courts of law. This master of the true understanding of the Self-in-God knows that the true self is so secure in a loving relationship with God that it can even bear false accusation with calm and equanimity.

> **To have lawsuits at all with one another is already a defeat for you. Why not rather be wronged? Why not rather be defrauded?** *Corinthians 6*

For this to happen we need to move beyond the calculating mind that seeks to judge and blame others to the contemplative mind that holds, accepts and refuses to blame and condemn. This is transformation.

The problem of the false self is very deep and may explain why many religious believers never get to grips with it. It is a subtle presence in our lives as it seeks to protect the ego by every means available including religion. In its religious form it can be one of the most difficult things to acknowledge. Jesus is fully aware of how deep-seated these roots of the false self are when he says:

> **If any want to become my followers, let them deny themselves and take up their cross and follow me. For those who want to save their life will lose it, and those who lose their life for my sake will find it.** *Matthew 16*

Jesus is pointing out that something has to be lost, to be let go of, to die, in order that we will find true and authentic life. He is making it very clear that this will be a painful process as it will strip off and uncover the outer layers we have built to protect our vulnerable, broken and wounded selves. He is not talking here about giving up chocolate or beer for Lent. He is challenging us to give up our self-centred, self-referenced existence. He is doing this so that we will find and discover a wholeness of life and an abundance of joy which are only available to those who have died to the false self and whose lives are now hidden with Christ in God.

At the heart of this struggle for believers is the religious false self which uses religion to prevent the very dying process that Jesus says is necessary. We fall into the trap of thinking that since we are believers everything is fine. No great change is demanded of us, certainly nothing as drastic as conversion. We may be very observant of our religious duties, attend church regularly, say our prayers, work for God in a variety of ways, but lack any sense of union with God. At the time of Jesus, the Pharisees and Scribes were outwardly very faithful followers of every aspect of the Law. They were the guardians of orthodoxy. Yet in the gospel we find these apparent paragons of virtue fighting Jesus on nearly every page. It is summed up perfectly in the opening lines of chapter fifteen in Luke's gospel:

> **Now all the tax-collectors and sinners were coming near to listen to him. And the Pharisees and the Scribes were grumbling and saying, this fellow welcomes sinners and eats with them.** *Luke 15*

The religious false self can be seen in righteous people who become very judgemental of others. This is one of the most off-putting aspects of religion. We love to compare ourselves with others. As we observe the duties of our religion and its practices we can look down on those who don't, what the gospel categorises as *tax-collectors and sinners*. This includes all those people of whom we disapprove. The false self loves to have God on its own terms. Although Jesus warns us not to judge others, the false self can only exist by judging others unfavourably, especially from a position of religious righteousness. As we will see in a later chapter, if we are truly to find the God, who is the forgiving and merciful Father of Jesus, then we have to lose this wonderful reputation we have built for ourselves. We have to let go of our egos in whatever form they take, especially our religious egos. In a very real sense we have to experience being lost if we are ever to be found by God. The tax-collectors, the prostitutes, and the sinners all instinctively knew and sensed this, which is why they were attracted to the presence of Jesus.

The religious false self thinks that we can only come into the presence of God if we are worthy – the only way to become worthy is by our best efforts at being *good* and *holy*. Nothing could be further from the truth! This is a huge shock to the religious false self. Our seeking after a good reputation in the eyes of others, our striving for moral perfection, is the very thing that has to die. Robert Mulholland Jr underlines this when he points out:

> **For those of us on an intentional spiritual journey, our awareness of the deadly and debilitating nature of the religious false self is essential. Rigorous religious practices, devoted discipleship, sacrificial service, deeper devotional activities may do nothing more than turn a nominally religious false self into a fanatically religious false self.[9]**

---

9 Robert Mulholland Jr *The Deeper Journey* (Inter Varsity Press Illinois 2006) p 48

This reveals the danger of a self-centred religious journey. It is not unusual today to see spirituality promoted in newspapers and colour supplements. The danger is that spirituality then becomes yet another consumer accessory, another aspect of the envied life-style. There is little evidence of *dying-to-self* in this postmodern spirituality.

Our reluctance to let go of our self-referenced lives is brilliantly described in the gospels. It is not just the Pharisees who fight Jesus on this issue. The same is true of his closest followers. When Jesus revealed to his apostles that he would have to experience rejection, suffering and crucifixion, they also would not accept it. This issue is so important for Jesus that the only time he addresses anyone with the name *Satan* in the gospels is when he rebukes Peter for trying to deflect him from this path.

We all have an understandable fear of suffering. We all fear losing control of our lives. The spiritual challenge is to overcome this fear by trusting in love. We can only really do this when we discard the false masks we hide behind to protect our vulnerable selves. When St Theresa of Avila wrote her spiritual classic, *The Interior Castle*, she made it very clear that the foundation of the castle is self-knowledge. Traditionally, we have been told that there are seven deadly sins. Recent developments like the Enneagram[10] have uncovered a largely hidden sin: the sin of fear. Fear of being wrong, fear of making mistakes, fear of not being part of the in-crowd, fear of not being promoted. What often passes for loyalty and obedience in the Church can be fear in disguise. The deepest fear of all is of a God whom I have not experienced at the core of my being as utterly loving and merciful. If I do not know who I really am, if I do not experience myself as beloved son/daughter I will not really know the God of Jesus.

Most institutions set great store by loyalty and obedience. We are always being advised not to rock the boat by those at the top. If we want to succeed and be popular we have to play the game and observe the rules. The God of Jesus on the other hand invited us into a spacious place of great freedom, the freedom of the children of God. There we are taught that God can reconcile everything, both the light and the dark in our lives. We have to accept our mixture of blessings, to carry the cross of knowing we are wounded and vulnerable, but that our names are written in heaven, that we are beloved of God.

Modern psychology tells us to get in touch with our feelings, with our anger, our sense of inadequacy, with our fear. Spirituality takes us to a deeper level by revealing why we need to get in touch with these feelings. It is to get in

---

10   System of character analysis, using nine types based on inner motivation

touch with love. That is the ultimate reality. That is the truth of who we are. From the first moment of my existence I have been loved unconditionally by God. There is simply no need to go on amassing external signs to shore up my sense of self-worth and value. Happiness is an inside job. Along with everyone else I have been created for intimate union with God. My true self can never be earned by acts of worthiness; it is pure gift and it is to a consideration of this gift that we will now turn.

Chapter 3 — The True Self

The inner self is not an ideal self, especially not an imaginary perfect creature fabricated to measure up to our compulsive need for greatness, heroism and infallibility. On the contrary, the real I is simply myself and nothing more. Nothing more and nothing less. Our self as we are in the eyes of God, to use Christian terms. Our self in all our uniqueness, dignity, littleness and ineffable greatness: the greatness we have received from God our Father and that we share with Him because He is our Father and in him we live and move and have our being.[11]

The true self, or the inner self, is the whole self, fully connected to the bigger picture, to the realm of spirit. It contrasts with the false, or small self, which is constantly needy and anxious. The false self is living outside of God, living autonomously, what St Paul describes as living in the *flesh*. We need to keep asking ourselves who we really are, and learning to live in our true and more spacious identity as beloved of God. The paradox is that we cannot create or produce the true self; it is pure gift, it simply has to be received. Nor do we receive it when we are winning and succeeding, but when we are losing and failing. You can see why Jesus spoke about the straight and narrow way. This kind of teaching goes right against all the trends of our contemporary culture which is geared to success and achievement. Success and achievement are not bad and, in fact, they are necessary for the first half of life. What I am addressing here is the agenda for the second half of life, the discovery that I have to let go of my ego, to get myself out of the way, to allow God to invade my being, to lose my (false) self in order to find my (true) self.

In contrasting flesh and spirit, it is important to understand that when Paul uses the word *spirit* he is not speaking about the Holy Spirit. That theology hadn't been developed in his time. He is speaking really about what we would call *grace*. This is the new reality that is at the heart of *The Kingdom of God*, at the heart of the good news, at the heart of everything that Jesus is talking about. Grace is the supreme and wonderful gift of God's love and mercy in our lives – and here is the whole point – in the lives of every single person. The difference is that some people are aware of it and some are not. This is not a denominational issue but is essentially about transformation. Being a spiritual person is not the same as being a pious, churchgoing person, or a religious

---

11   Thomas Merton *The Inner Experience* (Harper San Francisco 2003) p 11

person. It is an invasion of God into my life. It is the moment when I fall into the arms of a loving God who accepts every part of me, good and bad, strengths and weaknesses.

This invasion comes from outside of us, yet paradoxically, it is already within us. It is your deepest you. When you experience it – and no one else can experience it for you – you finally feel totally accepted, totally forgiven, totally found. It echoes the surprise of Jacob awaking from his dream at Bethel:

> **Surely the Lord is in this place – and I did not know it!**
> *Genesis 28* ·

This is the true revelation of my identity. Paul uses the word *adoption* to describe this reality. We didn't realise that we were part of God's family, now we have received the gift as adopted children. This inheritance is not something I have earned. I could never earn it or be worthy of it. All I can to do is to say, *Thank you*. Living in the true self leads to true and genuine joy; it frees us from the trap of *religion as duty*. You can see why Paul got so annoyed with the Church in Galatia for appearing to fall back precisely into that very trap:

> **Are you so foolish? Having started with the Spirit are you ending with the flesh? Did you experience so much for nothing? Does God supply you with the Spirit and work miracles among you by your doing the works of the law, or by your believing what you have heard?**
> *Galatians 3*

Why is it that Christians can lapse back into a performance-based religion of duty rather than enjoy the realm of grace and freedom? If we are honest with ourselves, we know that even though on our better days we may live in conscious awareness of God's love and mercy, we still fall back into our old ways. We find it difficult to shake off our sense of shame and inadequacy. This is the *drag effect* of original sin, which we never seem to shake off. We are no different from those Galatians. Although we have been found by God, we still have a tendency to get lost. Forgetting who we are in God, we fall back into the self-centred way of the needy false self that is constantly judging and comparing ourselves with others, the false self that is so easily hurt.

The amazing nature of God's love is now revealed. That moment, when we feel most *lost*, is the very point where God draws closest to us and finds us again and welcomes us home. The gospels make it crystal-clear that Jesus reaches out to the people who experienced themselves as lost and abandoned. He spends his time with them, eats with them and forgives them; he is described as the friend of tax-collectors and sinners. It is not the law-observant Pharisees who understand Jesus, but the poor, the weak, the wounded, the broken, the rejected ones – *the nobodies*. Having criticised the Galatians, Paul puts himself in the same category in his letter to the Romans:

> **I do not understand my own actions. For I do not do what I want, but I do the very thing I hate... for I know that nothing good dwells within me, that is, in my flesh. I can will what is right but I cannot do it.** *Romans 7*

If we are truly honest with ourselves, we all need to identify with what Paul is saying. We all know, deep-down, that however long we have tried to live good spiritual lives, no matter how often we have been to church, or said our prayers, we remain a mass of contradictions.

I recall a moment in my own experience which still remains painful for me some years later. A member of a community, in which I was living, told me very bluntly everything that was wrong with me. He put his finger on every fault I had – and a few more I wasn't aware of! It was brutal and painful, but the more I later reflected on and prayed about that pain, I also recognised its truth. At the time this was a very humiliating experience but it taught me something about the importance of failure and woundedess that I could never have learned from books or sermons. The one thing the false self doesn't want to lose is a good reputation, my desire to feel that I am getting it right, that I am a good example to others. This is the part of me that has to die.

We discover how the Paschal Mystery lies at the heart of the spiritual life. When I am made aware of my shortcomings and my inability to be always loving and compassionate then I reach a crucial stage in understanding how God loves me. When I fall back into the frustration that Paul describes, I learn that I cannot fix or control my spiritual life. I cannot make myself holy; I cannot transform myself. Any effort to try to remedy the situation would be an act of the false self that wants to be successful. Paul stresses that this is precisely how Christ transforms us from within. He dwells in our far from perfect selves. *He dwells in our false selves in the form of crucified love:*

> **While we were still sinners (trapped in our false selves) Christ died for us.** *Romans 5*

It is clear that the problem of the false self is resolved by the intimate presence of Christ's saving love. This is the very process of transformation. Our false self is taken into the death of Christ and transformed by him into a new and different life, which Paul describes as being in Christ or as a new creation. Robert Mulholland puts it this way:

> **Paul is saying that entering into the core of our false self with Christ is a cruciform experience. This is where the cross exists for us. The cross is grounded in the core of our false self, and it is by entering into the core of our false self that we experience the cruciform love of God in Christ. When we embrace the cross there, in our false self, we release that false self to the cross, to Christ, to the crucified One. In that release we begin to experience the power of his resurrection raising us out of the deadness of the false self into the wholeness of life in the image of Christ, life in loving union with God. That is, as we suffer with him, we are also glorified with him.[12]**

This is how we experience the saving, healing and forgiving love of God. We cannot save ourselves: we cannot get ourselves out of this self-centred existence. Christ does it for us. The false self will always resist this, even though Christ lives in us, even though we receive the Eucharist as food for our souls. So from time to time we slip back into the false, wounded, needy self. This is the journey of transformation, which is never complete this side of heaven. All we can do is desire it with true and genuine longing. The presence of Christ within us remains a crucified presence. Yet the paradox is that it is also the risen Christ within us who shares his glory with us. In the great mystery of Incarnation we see God doing everything he can to unite matter and spirit. The problem for religious believers is that we want to abandon our wounded humanity and go straight to God, to reach upwards for spirit. Instead of embracing and owning our flawed humanity, we want to deny it, and the biggest disguise is through the cloak of religion.

Our world today is greatly threatened by religious extremism. We see it in radical Islamists and also in Christian fundamentalists, and in other religious extremists. The fundamentalist attaches himself to God; everything is done in the name of God. Once this happens, all thinking stops. There is no need for any effort at dialogue with other points of view. The fundamentalists have all the truth they need, and they are so convinced that, in the extreme form, they are prepared to kill anyone who does not share their narrow, perverted view of the truth. This is the world of the suicide bomber, of the terrorist prepared to commit mass murder of innocent civilians. In this simplistic world of unthinking

---

12 M Robert Mulholland Jr *The Deeper Journey* (Inter Varsity Press Illinois 2006) p 78-79

religious conviction, there is no need for personal conversion, for the difficult task of denying my false self. All the anger and pain from living in an imperfect world can then be projected onto an enemy, who will bear all of the suffering. This mindset that is prepared to kill others in the name of God is the most perverted sign of the false self.

Living in the true self creates a very different world. It is a spacious loving place, rather than narrow and threatening. The world of the true self is so big that it can embrace everything, especially the evil, the broken, the damaged, the flawed part of our human existence. Here everything belongs, everything can be used by God, everything can be transformed, especially my faults and weaknesses. Here the wound becomes sacred. This is the essence of transformation.

I have already referred to God as the great recycler. The more I think about recycling, the more I see it as a wonderful image for God, who takes all aspects of our lives and transforms them into good. This is the great Paschal cycle of death and resurrection. Anything in my life that I want to reject, to deny, or to throw away, God picks up and transforms. This is the nature of cruciform love. Holiness as transformation has nothing to do with striving after moral purity and perfection. That is a task which the false self is all too happy to take up and to feel good about. The true self doesn't reject anything because God doesn't reject anything. The true self doesn't reject the false self; it embraces it and includes it. It leads the false self into the bigger picture where life and love and meaning don't have to be created entirely by me as an individual. All I have to do is to participate in the mystery of death and glory which comes from beyond me, of which I am only a small part.

Good religion always leads us into the bigger picture: *The Kingdom of God*. This is the world of spirit and of grace. It is the world of gift and of mercy. It is not interested in judging and comparing. It is freed from the compulsions of the self-centred life. The false self alone is simply not capable of living the mystery of sin and glory which lies at the heart of all human experience.

The true self is your true identity, who you are in God. The insecure false self always wants to ignore and exclude the dark side of life. The fundamentalist cannot cope with any doubt or ambiguity. We see this in many Christians who get so easily upset by what they judge as *imperfect* behaviour, *imperfect* liturgical performance, or *imperfect* theology. Jesus spent very little time and energy on imperfect behaviour. Rather than condemn and expel it, he forgave and healed anyone who was humble enough to admit any form of need. His problem was with those who were so convinced of their moral and religious righteousness that they saw no need to ask for any kind of healing or forgiveness. On almost every page of the gospel the compassion of Jesus is met by the unforgiving moral righteousness of the Scribe and the Pharisee.

In the true self, there is no narrow-mindedness or judgementalism. When you are in the presence of someone who is living in the true self you see a very attractive soulfulness, a larger than life character, someone who doesn't take himself or herself too seriously. They know that there is no longer any need to hate their enemies, or hate themselves. Everything is embraced, blessed and forgiven. On a visit to Hong Kong, some years ago, I was introduced to two amazing Salesian priests. Both had been imprisoned by Chinese communists for twenty seven years. During that time they had no contact with their Salesian community, their families, or any friends. They were not allowed to carry any religious picture or symbol, such as a crucifix, rosary, or holy picture. I just wondered how they had managed to sustain and deepen their faith during those long years of imprisonment and isolation. It was a privilege to be in the same room as these men who harboured no resentment or anger, but radiated an extraordinary serenity and peace. In one sense their lives and energy had been lost to the Church yet they had found God at the deepest level of their souls. This meeting made a deep impression on me and reminded me that we don't convert anyone by what we know or do; what we have to share is *who we are*.

Living in the true self leads into a place of wisdom rather than knowledge. There are many very clever people whose lives are trapped in the false ego-centred self, and there are many uneducated people who live in a largeness of soul and spirit. Such people have learned and been transformed not by moral or intellectual purity, but by the wisdom of the wound. They know what it is like to be both lost and found.

This is a different kind of knowing. The false self is the domain of the calculative mind, the mind that is obsessed with the need to control and dominate reality, to bend reality to my own self-referenced agenda. Even with all the power and money imaginable, this is a doomed project and when it fails before the intractable problems of life, then I seek to find someone else to blame. The false self is determined to try to fix reality. The true self, on the other hand, lives in the contemplative gaze and we will examine this more in the next chapter. Suffice to say that the contemplative mind looks at reality from a much more centred place, from a deeper source of life. Contemplation is therefore *the ability to see, to see what is,* without wanting to judge it or fix it. This is far from passivity and indifference in the face of the many injustices in life. On the contrary, the true self is deeply aware of the dignity of all human life and the need to protect that dignity and promote it. The deeper we penetrate the mystery of God's love living within us the more we understand that everyone else shares in this love. This is true communion with God and with all things. With this contemplative mentality, any action for justice is rooted not just in anger, however righteous, but from compassion and an awareness of my own complicity in the injustice I see around me. Rather than punish the perpetrators of injustice it seeks wherever possible to forgive and to invite all sides to build a more just and human future.

The true self helps me to realise that there are some things that cannot be changed. There is no such thing as a perfect society, perfect community, perfect family or perfect Church. Of course, we must work to improve whatever we can but at the end of the day we meet and own the inevitable shadow-side of human behaviour. The very word *religion* comes from the Latin, *re-ligio*, and reminds us of the need to put everything together, to overcome all divisions by inclusion not by exclusion. We are told in the letter to the Ephesians that God's plan and purpose is to gather up and unite all things both in heaven and on earth. The task of good religion is therefore to bring together what has been divided. It overcomes the dualism that has bedevilled us for so long and unites heaven and earth, male and female, saint and sinner, sin and salvation, crucifixion and resurrection, death and life. The great saints and mystics are the ones who understand this intuitively.

There are some things that cannot be fixed in this imperfect world in which we live and the true self provides space to accept the inconsistencies and the flaws of human existence. Rather than seek to fix the flaws of others the true self allows me to accept the flaws within myself. The great defeat of the ego-centred false self is that I have to acknowledge my own woundedness and admit that I alone cannot fix this problem. I have to allow the healing touch of Christ within me. All I have to do is to stay connected, to stay in relationship, to stay in union and know that Christ will transform me in his time and in his way.

Although the spirit of God comes from beyond us, at the same time it is already implanted in us. As Paul makes clear:

You are not in the flesh; you are in the Spirit, since the Spirit of God dwells in you. *Romans 8*

In John's Gospel, Jesus himself tells us that he and his Father will make their home in us. So the spirit without connects with the spirit within. It is all about connection. It is as if we already have a taste of this influx of new life that makes us into a new creation, that reveals our true identity. It is the give-and-take and desire for mutuality that the love God has planted in us. This gift of grace is not the result of any moral behaviour of ours; all our moral behaviour flows from the recognition of our true identity: if this is who you are – a temple of the spirit – then behave accordingly. God's love and spirit is the creative life-force in all human beings. When we pray it is God praying within us. If I get the urge to pray, it is the spirit within me, prompting me. All I can do is provide the connection, stay rooted to the vine as Jesus teaches. This is the *Yes of faith*, an act of trust in God that is deeper than any credal affirmation.

The great human paradox is carrying the mystery of who I am – someone who lives by the selfish agenda of the false self and, at the same time, someone who exists in union with God. This is the mystery of the Cross and Resurrection, not as a doctrine which I assent to in my head, but as a daily reality of who I am. Paul advises us to assent to this presence of God's love at the very core of our being. By slowly dying to the false agenda, the life of God becomes manifest in our souls and transforms all our relationships:

> **Others are no longer valued for the ways they enhance our agenda or devalued for the ways they thwart our agenda. Others can no longer be pawns in our game, objects for the fulfilment of our desires or enemies to be demonised and destroyed. Every person becomes one whom God loves and for whom God's grace is constantly poured out. We are to be the sister and brother through whom God's grace touches the other.**[13]

The spirit is our very ability to love. It is not something that starts with us; it is something that is done to us. Mary understood this in her famous, reply to the angel, *Let it be!* In his passage about the gifts in his first letter to the Corinthians, Paul lists all the gifts of the good Christian life and then goes on to say that they all mean nothing unless they are done with love.

In recent years, I have preached a number of retreats in different parts of the world. I am always touched when someone comes up to me after a talk and says, *That really resonated with me deep down.* I think this is because we all know this at a deep level of soul and the purpose of preaching is to bring that reality alive. Preaching at times has a negative image for many. Too often we preachers are simply attacking others, pointing out their faults, whereas true preaching should awaken the hearts and souls of others to their true identity, to their true selves. It is after all supposed to be good news not bad news.

---

13   M Robert Mulholland Jr *The Deeper Journey* (Inter Varsity Press Illinois 2006) p 107

The pull of the false self will always be there. One of the clear signs of its presence is how often I take offence. The false self is always needy and easily hurt. Another indication is the lack of a sense of humour. If I cannot laugh at myself, or allow others to tease me then I am probably taking myself far too seriously, which is exactly what the false self does all the time. The true self leads us into a landscape of joy and real contentment. It has found the basis of all happiness. This is the eternal life that John's Gospel reminds us is a present gift. Too often, we Christians are guilty of projecting everything into the future. The message seems to be that if we can just put up with life's miseries and disappointments we will eventually be happy in heaven. This is to seriously underestimate the importance of the Incarnation, of the *now*. The great patterns of life and death, of sorrow and joy, of transformation are happening in our daily lives. The Bible has different ways of describing this foundational happiness: the true vine, the new covenant, the new creation, your names are written in heaven. It is all about grace.

The genius of St Paul is that he names the great spiritual problem: the confusing of religion and observance of the law with spirit. At times, we get caught up in language, beliefs, and observances and forget the great mystery of transformation for which we have been created. There are two great means of reminding ourselves of this mystery of death and resurrection working itself out in our world and in our lives. These are prayer and service of our neighbour. Once we discover our foundational identity we are led to a place where God always brings life out of death. We learn to experience this in our poverty, which we bring before God in prayer, and in the poverty of those in need. What we find in both places is not just a God who looks on sympathetically, but a God who actually identifies with what is broken and rejected. That is the mystery of the Cross, the place where our real life is found. God really is the great recycler.

Chapter 4 – Standing on your own two feet

We are at the dawn of a new consciousness, a radically fresh approach to our life as the human family in a fragile world.[14]

As the twentieth century drew to a close, a newspaper asked people to choose what they considered to be its most significant event. The most popular choice was the landing on the moon by American astronauts in July 1969. If I had been asked I would have chosen two events. The first was connected to the Apollo moon programme, but not the actual landing. For me the most significant moment was seeing those amazing pictures of planet Earth from space. In the immense blackness of space, we saw the tiny, rather fragile, but incredibly beautiful planet that we all share. In one of the Apollo flights, the astronauts had to go behind the moon for the first time. For twenty minutes, they were out of contact with Mission Control in Houston. When they broke radio silence one of them was reading from the book of Genesis, *In the beginning, God created the heavens and the earth*. When questioned about this later, he said he felt it was the only appropriate way to describe what he was seeing.

My second highly significant moment occurred in 1988 when Pope John Paul II gathered the leaders of the world religions with him at Assisi to pray for peace. The rise of religious extremism and fundamentalism, since then, has only underlined the prophetic nature and importance of that event. The two events are deeply connected in that they reveal the only way forward in an increasingly vulnerable and fragile world. Rabbi Jonathon Sacks puts it succinctly:

Because each of us has something someone else lacks, and we each lack something someone else has, we gain by interaction.[15]

We have to find ways to come together. Our planet is so fragile and our modern weaponry is so destructive, that we either find ways of understanding and respecting differences of faith, of race, of political views, or we will go on killing each other. This issue is very urgent in our day. I think it is made more difficult by the feeling that we have lost our way in the world. The issues are also so big that at times we can feel overwhelmed. No political leader seems

---

14   Wayne Teasdale *The Mystic Heart* (New World Library CA 2001) p 4

15   Jonathon Sacks *The Dignity of Difference* (Continuum, London 2002) p 15

able to articulate them for us. Efforts to reach out to understand and interact with others are drowned out by the violence of the War on Terror. I want to suggest that if we are to make any contribution to greater understanding and peace in our world we have to make the inner journey. The journey to reach out to others, the journey without, has to be rooted in the journey within.[16]

On the day he died, Thomas Merton told a very revealing story. He was speaking at a meeting of Christian and Buddhist monks and nuns in Bangkok. He related how the people of Tibet were fleeing from Chinese persecution. Chogyam Trungpa Rinpoche, having been cut off from his monastery, took refuge in a village with a peasant family. Completely lost and bewildered he sent a request for help and advice to a nearby abbot friend. In desperation, he asked what he was supposed to do. His friend gave the enigmatic answer: *From now on we all have to stand on our own two feet.* Merton thought that the answer was very significant. What was he getting at?

I think he was addressing the fact that many of us don't know who we really are. Many religious people attach themselves to religious institutions. Now we need religious institutions, but they cannot make the spiritual journey for us. Institutions get us started but they will not get us all the way home. The early books of the Bible are clearly setting out the structure of the Jewish faith. Books like Deuteronomy and Leviticus deal with the beginnings of religious identity. They are full of detailed laws and rituals.

This is an important stage in religious development and it provides a much-needed sense of boundaries, and a moral code to live by. It makes it clear who belongs and who doesn't, who is in and who is out. This is what can be termed the masculine structure of religion, important and necessary, but not the whole picture.

The problem is that over-identification with the institution leads to a largely external piety, a conformity to rules and regulations. Identifying with the institution also means that I cannot be tied to its apron strings: I don't need to grow up; the institution does it all for me. Much of the resistance of the Pharisees and Scribes to the message of Jesus found expression in this false sense of identity. They described themselves as children of Abraham, implying that they had nothing to learn from Jesus. They knew it all. This is how religion gets distorted by the false self. It will do everything to block and avoid genuine conversion and transformation. All too often, we Catholics have done just that: we are Catholics, we have the truth, we don't need to change, everybody else does. At times the Church has allowed this rather childish attitude, even

---

16 Michael Cunningham *Within & Without* (Don Bosco Publications 2003)

encouraged it. I think this is a problem with all institutions. They encourage control and order.

The most spiritually-aware of the Jewish people were conscious of this danger and so the early books of law and ritual in the Bible are followed by a very different kind of literature. These are the prophetic books and look at religion from a very different perspective. The prophets reminded the Jewish people that religion wasn't just about observance of the law and ritual. The prophets looked at everything from the perspective of the poor. They asked the question, *What was the purpose of a detailed following of the law and regular liturgical worship if the poor were being neglected?* The prophets put their finger on the central problem, which Jesus reiterated later, that it is perfectly possible to follow the letter of the law, with a heart that remains closed and indifferent to the sufferings of the poor and vulnerable. The prophets made the clear and non-negotiable link between private and public religion. The two cannot be separated if spirituality is to remain authentic.

They made an even deeper observation. They underlined, what St Paul made clear in describing his own behaviour in the letter to the Romans, that no one individual, however good or holy, could keep every aspect of the law of God. None of us is perfect and we never will be. This prophetic insight radically undermined the whole structure of the false self, especially in its religious form.

The temptation of first-stage religion, the observance of what might be termed external rules and practices, is that I can hide my personal failure and weaknesses in the strength of the institution. Membership becomes much more important than transformation. I remember an incident in my childhood when I had been laughing at members of the Salvation Army Band in my home town of Radcliffe in Lancashire. My Dad was quick to point out the error of my ways, and reminded me that I should never laugh at anybody or any organisation that was working for the poor. Unbeknown to me at the time, my father was hinting at the need for me to move from stage-one to stage-two spirituality. My father was a traditional working-class Catholic, who had to leave school for the world of work at the age of twelve when his father died. He never received anything like the educational opportunities that I have been fortunate to enjoy, but he knew what mattered: he lived the gospel.

Membership is important and we all need to start there. Parents and teachers will be well aware of the need for discipline, rules, and order in bringing up and educating the young. We all have to start conservative, but we cannot stay there. It is interesting to see that the message of the prophets was far from popular. Jesus himself referred to this when he met so much resistance to his good news of forgiveness and compassion for the poor. It is also interesting to see how Jesus both admired yet distanced himself from the man he called the greatest of the prophets, John the Baptist. None of the prophets, even John, are perfect. They exemplify the spiritual problem at the heart of the social justice agenda. As Richard Rohr says:

To be prophets we must first see in ourselves what we see in others: good and bad.[17]

It has to include both, good and bad, which leads to an amazing humility rather than any kind of righteous arrogance. Some of the biblical prophets can be seen moving from a deep consciousness of God to a real desire for vengeance and punishment. We see it in figures such as Elijah and Jonah and we see it in the preaching of John the Baptist. He speaks of gathering the wheat while the chaff is burnt in unquenchable fire. He warns that every tree that does not bear fruit will be cut down and thrown into the fire. Now Jesus has high praise for John the Baptist: *no man born of woman is greater than he* – yet he immediately adds that *the least in the kingdom is greater*. Jesus is suggesting that mere prophetic righteousness still lacks something. Some of John's contemporaries described him as a new Elijah. Both had this great zeal for God, but both had something of the fanaticism of the first-stage believer who wants to create a clear identity between those who belong and those who do not.

Healthy biblical religion was able to hold and honour the place of law and ritual, without losing an awareness of the needs of the poor. This struggle between what might be called law and prophets reached a new consciousness and integration in the Wisdom literature.[18] These writers recognised that both observance of the law and concern for the poor have to be lived from the heart, from a place of deep compassion. The genius of Wisdom literature is that it recognises the great spiritual maxim that no one else is my problem. I have to be transformed. For this to happen, I cannot sit in judgement of my neighbour as I carry out the externals of my faith, and I cannot sit in judgement of my neighbour as I work on behalf of the poor. This brings me back to the foundational question of who I am. Self-acceptance is basic and foundational and that means accepting all that I am and refusing to deny my shadow-side and push it on to someone else.

---

17 Richard Rohr *Everything Belongs* (Crossroad Publishing Company NY 2003) p 174

18 Wisdom literature - any of the biblical books e g Proverbs, Ecclesiastes, Song of Songs, that are considered to contain wisdom.

I have to grow up and make the journey that Jesus says is essential, the dying and rising that is the Paschal Mystery. It is clear that many people in our world today are experiencing pain. We see it in the violence, the hatred, and the desire to identify an enemy. Identifying an enemy is always universally popular. In the west, we see it in the psychic pain that many experience in broken relationships. Some find their identity and energy in fighting an enemy. Oppositional energy certainly works in the short-term. I remember watching an interview with a mid-west farmer on the eve of a US presidential election. He outlined his choice and gave the reason: this candidate identifies our enemy, we know who we are against. Sadly this is all too common in our world. It might work in the short-term, but spiritually it is bankrupt as it asks my enemy to do all the changing while I remain the same.

Merton is putting his finger on a key spiritual challenge, by asking us to stand on our own two feet. My task is to be transformed by growing up and accepting who I am. This involves getting rid of my masks and the social games that force others to change while I stay as I am; preserving my good name and reputation. I cannot hide behind the fact of my denominational membership. Denominational membership alone can be a trap for the false self. Too much religion today operates at the level of cultural identity. Attachment to a group is a very subtle way of protecting the ego, especially the group ego. Every institution has its shadow side. When the Catholic Church was first hit by the scandal of child abuse, it emerged that, in the past, the instinctive reaction of many bishops had been to deny the problem and simply move clergy to a different area.

I have to say, I am proud to be a Catholic and so grateful for what my mother and father passed on to me. I feel genuinely sorry for those who no longer feel able to identify with the institutional Church. We all need ritual in our lives to touch those parts of our souls that go beyond the humdrum and the mundane and remind us where we have come from and where we are going. Without religious ritual, the sacred disappears from our lives and that may account for the general coarsening of the spirit that we see in so much of what counts as popular entertainment. When Vatican II called for renewal in the Church, we might have thought it just needed some cosmetic changes. Maybe like political parties, we thought that evangelisation was all a matter of presentation. Some of the renewal movements like charismatic prayer groups just wanted to live the joyous aspect of the faith. Healing ministry thought it could take away the pain and brokenness of life. Wherever there is light, there is also a shadow cast and this is what has emerged very painfully in recent years. The Church cannot just preach the Paschal Mystery; it has to make the painful journey itself to new life.

Another example of the Church's shadow is parochialism. Because of the shortage of clergy, many dioceses in the western world are engaged in re-structuring. This is a painful process and involves the amalgamating of parishes and the closing of churches. The bishops are being courageous in facing up to these issues but many of the faithful resist the process. Re-structuring is fine in theory, as long as it does not mean *my* church, *my* parish, *my* school. The old catechisms used to remind us that the word *catholic* meant *universal*, but for too many, we substitute *parochial* for *universal*. There seems to be little awareness of the bigger picture.

Tradition is an essential part of any institution. The problem is with traditionalism, which is usually selective. A resistance to change often disguises *refusal to change*, because I don't want to move outside my comfort zone. Mature spirituality has a sense of the world dimension of genuine faith, of its unity and its diversity. We speak of a vocation crisis, but the western Church has probably had too many priests for too long now. It has led to a rather top-heavy and an over-clericalised Church which has not always produced an adult spirituality. When the civil war was raging in Liberia, in West Africa, a few years ago I remember going with some of my fellow Salesians to visit a part of the country which had been in rebel hands. We got permission to travel through this area, although the journey was not without its hazards and threats. We finally reached a parish where there had been no priest for two or three years. We met a young catechist who with his wife had kept alive a vibrant community. They gathered every Sunday to read from the scriptures and to sing their hymns. I was very struck by the life and goodness of that little group who really had learned how to stand on their own two feet. I am not suggesting that this is an ideal situation; the Eucharist is such a vital part of our Christian way of life, but the life and enthusiasm of this group contrasted with some congregations I have encountered, which were hardly life-giving. The shortage of vocations really is asking us to grow a much more lay centred and less clerical Church, which means that we need an adult laity with an adult spirituality to carry this forward.

This adult spirituality has to embrace the shadow-side of the Church, as much as it has to embrace the shadow-side of our own personal lives. In the complex world in which we find ourselves, we can no longer simply identify ourselves with our institutional labels. I have been focusing on the Catholic Church to which I belong, but this is true of all institutions. In a recent speech, the Pope upset the Muslim community by quoting a rather obscure Byzantine emperor who denigrated the prophet Mohammed. The Pope had the courage to apologise indicating his real and genuine respect for the Muslim faith. Some of his defenders argued that the people hadn't studied the whole of the Pope's lecture. But in these days of instant and twenty-four hour media coverage the

Pope was surely right to say that he hadn't intended to give any offence. When John Paul II stood together with the leaders of all the world's faiths, he began a new relationship where we could move from being rivals to seeing ourselves as fellow-pilgrims and fellow-searchers.

The Biblical Wisdom tradition teaches all of us that religion is not about who is right and who is wrong, about who is superior and who is inferior, but that everything comes down to love and compassion, to what is in the heart. In the Catholic Church, we have always prided ourselves on being a strong institution. Our leadership has been hierarchical and exclusively male. We have counted our numbers and gloried in our size. We valued unthinking obedience and our teaching has been heavily moral in content. I have tried to argue in this book that morality is not prior to but follows on from ontology (who we are), our being. We have produced an institution which too often valued external behaviour rather than inner experience.

I am conscious that I am writing these words on the feast of St Vincent de Paul, one of the most popular saints in the Church. Nearly every parish has an SVP group reminding us that the church must be concerned with the poor. Vincent was ordained at the age of nineteen, and in many ways, his choice of the priesthood was linked with the idea of enhancing his career prospects. He wasn't really in touch with his inner life and in his early years he showed little interest in the poor. Then in his mid-twenties he underwent a real conversion when he was first made prisoner in North Africa where he was seeking to recover some money which had been stolen from him. Then he underwent a three-year-long spiritual crisis of faith. He emerged from these experiences a very changed man, with his faith greatly strengthened. He had grown from someone who worked for God to becoming someone who was in love with God. He had met God's unconditional and unmerited love at the very core of his being, mediated through the experience of his own weakness and brokenness. He had experienced the compassion of God and now all he could do was to behave towards the poor in the way that God had behaved towards him. He had lost the arrogance of his youth and found the wisdom of vulnerability.

Biblical religion doesn't provide a set of answers to support the religious ego in its sense of superiority. Biblical religion is a process, a journey of death and resurrection, one already mapped out for us by Jesus, who doesn't tell us to worship him but to follow him. Vincent de Paul, like all the saints and the mystics, followed this path of descent. Suffering in itself is not a good thing but it seems to be the only thing that really destabilises the ego. This is the way to discovering the true self which is always a gift. The culture of the past that handed on the faith to the next generation has largely gone. We are in a radically new situation. Many in the Church grieve over what we have lost. We look back with nostalgia to a lost world of May processions, Friday fasts, and Mass in Latin. That world is very unlikely to return. Conservative Catholics feel that we have lost our identity, that which distinguished us from other Christians, let alone the members of other faiths, such as Islam or Hinduism.

While some grieving for what we have lost is understandable we forget that Jesus said, *Let the dead bury the dead.* We have to find and discover where God is speaking and challenging us today. This is the world of the tiny and fragile planet Earth seen from space in all its vulnerability. It is the world of many faiths, of many paths to God as seen in that memorable gathering in Assisi. It is the world in which faith can no longer be passed on *en masse* by an institution. It has to be a genuine personal experience. We have to learn in Merton's words to stand on our own two feet. This does not mean that we stand alone in our religious identity. That is the world of the false self. Everything is relational, we go to God with others; but it is a relationship of mutual giving and receiving. We can no longer look down on others from our position of Catholic superiority. Our work for justice has to be truly collaborative and humble as we stand with all people of goodwill against the exploitation of the poor.

Biblical religion at its best honours all three key elements in spirituality. Jesus exemplifies all three dimensions. He knew the importance of tradition, law, boundaries, morality, ritual and doctrine:

> **Do not think that I have come to abolish the law or the prophets; I have come not to abolish but to fulfil.**
> *Matthew 5*

He reveals that purpose in the way he describes his mission on behalf of the poor:

> **The Spirit of the Lord is upon me, because he has anointed me to bring good news to the poor. He has sent me to proclaim release to the captives and recovery of sight to the blind, to let the oppressed go free.** *Luke 4*

He aligns himself fully with the prophetic tradition that sees the law fulfilled in works of justice for the outcasts, the broken ones, those in need of liberation. He then places himself within the wisdom tradition by revealing a God who seeks mercy not sacrifice, who seeks compassion not vengeance and punishment. He teaches his followers to forgive seventy times seven, to love the enemy, to welcome the stranger; to go beyond our immediate circle of family, of Church, of nation.

The religion of Jesus is a religion of the heart. That is why, while respecting the law, he frequently goes beyond it – *you have heard it said but I say to you.* He even goes beyond the desire of some who are in the prophetic tradition, to make distinctions between the just and the unjust, the worthy and the unworthy. This is clearly the agenda of the religious false self that believers of many religions are influenced by. Jesus invites us to a much bigger space, where the true self lives. Here all groups are included and there are no exceptions because it is the realm of love.

Only with a truly adult spirituality can we understand this, which is why Merton says it is so vital for the world in which we live. As we mourn what seemed like halcyon days in the Church, maybe we can recognise that the only way forward is to enter the Paschal journey of Jesus. We have to let go of our certainties and the easy answers of a more adolescent spirituality and allow ourselves to be transformed by the breath of the Holy Spirit in these times. This calls for an honest acceptance of ourselves with our vulnerabilities and weaknesses, a willingness to work with people and believers who are different from us, and not be afraid of our wounds. St Augustine once said, *In my deepest wound I see your glory and it dazzles me.* If we can learn to identify with those words of wisdom we will have truly found the One we have been looking for.

Chapter 5 — Losing My Religion

It is precisely in the face of the other, the face of the victims, that Jesus reveals himself as the Other. From the perspective of the Risen One, the fundamental open attitude is profoundly characterised by sensitivity towards the poor, the weak and the rejected.[19]

In 1984, the Louvain-based European Values Study under the leadership of Jan Kerkhofs published its findings under the title, *The Silent Turn*. It indicated that Belgium was turning its back on its traditional Roman Catholic identity. In 1992 the same group published a further study, *The Accelerated Turn*, claiming that the changes identified in the first study were accelerating. The 2000 study, *Lost Certainty*, suggested that the rejection of traditional Catholicism was complete. In the process of a few years Belgium had changed from a Roman Catholic society to a secular one. A similar pattern can be discerned in other Western European countries. Some may recall the alarm of the Vatican when European nations refused to include Christianity in the new European Constitution. A few years ago, the American pop group R.E.M. had a hit record *Losing my Religion*, describing the abandonment of an ancient tradition. A common theme of many people today from as far apart as the United States, Europe, and Australia is summed up in the remark, *I am not very interested in formal religion, I don't go to church, but I am interested in spirituality*. What is going on? What has happened in our western world that has led to this split between the structure and form of religious belief and the emotional core at the heart of that belief? Can we describe what is being lost and what is being found in this feature of our times?

We are living today in what can be described as *liminal times*. Liminal time is threshold time. We are leaving behind the culture of modernity and not sure what we are replacing it with. Even the very word postmodern is a negative. It is a time of profound and rapid change affecting all aspects of our lives. It breeds a kind of trauma and shock that brings everything into question. What once seemed secure and stable, no longer provides that kind of comfort and reassurance. We are at the threshold of something new but it hasn't clearly emerged yet. Hence the confusion and fear. In a stable society traditional forms of handing on cultural and religious values form the unquestioned background to life. Our postmodern world has rejected all such explanations. For postmodern men and women there is no such thing as a Master Narrative that explains everything. Ours is a deconstructed society in which no big

---

19   Lieven Boeve *Interrupting Tradition* (Peeters Press Louvain 2003) p 137

explanations are acceptable. We have rejected the bigger picture, the great pattern, and we are lost in a sea of individualism where the strong and the powerful hold sway. Historians point out that in any period of profound cultural change the same symptoms occur: loss of meaning, alienation, growth in violent crime, social and family breakdown and – especially in this current crisis – loss of religious faith and practice. The loss touches our souls.

The false dawn of the modern world that promised a rational paradise for people freed from religious authoritarianism has long since faded from view. The modern scientific mind thought that it could do whatever it wanted and solve all the problems of humanity. Education would lead people into this earthly paradise. The fact that the holocaust erupted in one of the most educated cultures was a severe jolt to such optimism. Two major world wars, and the countless deaths provoked by the rise of communism and fascism led to a real lack of belief and trust in all institutions and authority structures. Religious authority also felt the force of this sceptical wind that was sweeping across the western world. The United States might have felt these cultural forces later than Europe but in the 1960s and 70s, it too was dragged into the postmodern world with the Vietnam War, the assassination of the Kennedy brothers and Martin Luther King, the race-riots and the struggles of the civil rights movement, Watergate and the threatened impeachment of Richard Nixon. The promised peace dividend at the end of the cold war has evaporated before the onset of fundamentalist terrorism. The liberal secular west finds itself baffled by the violence and the energy behind international terrorism and the rise of the suicide bomber.

The cultural air seems bleak and wintry. In the past, religion might have provided a safe place from which to begin the reconstruction of society. Today, it seems to be just as helpless as any other carrier of meaning. It really is *every man for himself* with each individual having to construct his or her own world of meaning:

> **The soul, the psyche, human relationships seem at this point to be destabilising almost at an exponential rate. Our society is producing very many unhappy people and unhealthy people. The spread of violence everywhere in society is frightening. We're seeing that the postmodern mind is a deconstructed worldview. It does not know what it is for, as much as it knows what it is against and what it fears.[20]**

---

20   Richard Rohr *Hope Against Darkness* (St Anthony Messenger Press 2001) p 6

As a society we are living with a real sense of loss. Reason, science and technology have not delivered the earthly paradise they promised. The problem for faith groups is that very few of us are convinced that religion can ever again lead us either back to the Garden of Eden or forward to the Promised Land. The only believers with real conviction appear to be the fundamentalists of either right or left. Most tolerant, rational, and fair-minded people recoil in horror.

Religious leaders are, not surprisingly, struggling to react to this bleak landscape. Roman Catholicism has been traditionally identified with a strong and hierarchical leadership that provided certainty and called for obedience from the faithful. Such an authoritarian institution is particularly vulnerable in a world that ignores institutions and seeks meaning somewhere else. The Catholic Church has been further weakened and wounded by the scandal of child abuse. It is one thing for individual clergy to be found guilty of such abhorrent actions – although it inevitably calls into question all formation programmes in seminaries and houses of formation – but it also undermines the very structures of authority since those very structures often sought to deny and conceal the crimes rather than deal with them honestly. On the wider issue of sexuality the Church's teaching on birth control, on co-habitation, and on homosexuality has further weakened its grip on the faithful, especially the young.

While the Church has lost much of its power and influence in the secular west, the family has at the same time been coming under attack. In a consumer society, the idea of choice reigns supreme. Choice extends through every aspect of contemporary society, not just in the area of goods and services but also in the area of moral choice. Postmodern society rejects all claims of objective truth, replacing them with the personal choice of each individual. All choices are available within the one proviso that it doesn't hurt anybody, whatever that might mean. The intangible nature of that claim is revealed by the ever-burgeoning world of litigation and claims for compensation including a whole range of personal injuries. The institution of the family has also fallen victim to this new world of relativism and short-termism. Human rights – especially the right to do what I want to do – are rarely linked with human responsibility and children are the victims of parental breakdown and separation. The family has joined religion as a market commodity.

The handing-on of any kind of tradition in this climate is very problematic. A mother, inquiring about the baptism of her child, recently asked one of the priests in my Salesian community in Liverpool, *Will it be a Requiem Mass?* Catholic schools have long found themselves under criticism by parish clergy for the failure of schools to produce practising Catholics. I recently quizzed a group of Year 10 students in a Catholic high school about the basics of the Christmas story. Their ignorance didn't surprise me and I am not criticising their teachers. I spent many years in that very difficult task. The ignorance of the Christmas story is taking place in a culture which has transformed the Christmas season from a religious festival into the high point of the consumer year. Political correctness often seeks to deny any public reference to the birth of Christ.

The question of how to hand on traditional teaching and practices in such a climate reaches right across postmodern culture. Religion is simply one aspect of this crisis. Belgian theologian Lieven Boeve describes the problem:

> **Can the flagging and ineffectual transmission of the Christian tradition guarantee the survival of the Christian narrative? For decades Christians have found themselves increasingly unable to fruitfully initiate the following generations into the Christian faith. As such the very transmission of the tradition as such is in serious danger. The still fairly reasonable percentages of people who participate in the 'rites of passage' (baptism, confirmation, marriage, funeral) tend to obscure the reality of the situation. Studies have shown that secularisation is continuing at a faster pace than ever before and not only with respect to people's faith engagement and their church involvement. Culture itself is undergoing a process of detraditionalisation.[21]**

Lieven Boeve suggests that the gap between contemporary culture and the Christian faith is continuing to widen. He argues that every new context challenges the Christian tradition to find new ways to communicate its meaning. Handing on the tradition alone will get us nowhere. Accommodating it to the new culture is equally fruitless. What is needed, he suggests, is a new and genuine dialogue between tradition and culture. He points out that Jesus is the supreme example of how to do this in the way that he spoke of God in an incredibly open way and constantly challenged his own Jewish tradition to an ever expanding openness. In this way he was demonstrating the vitality and strength of the tradition and repeatedly challenged the Scribes and Pharisees who had locked the tradition into a rigid conformity and legalism.

American scripture scholar Walter Breuggemann also suggests the need to find new and more creative ways of living the Christian tradition. He compares

---

21   Lieven Boeve *Interrupting Tradition* (Peeters Press Louvain 2003) p 4-5

American culture with its rampant consumerism and global outreach to the kind of royal consciousness that in biblical times stifled and domesticated the radical dream of Moses. He identifies the contemporary malaise as inducing numbness that paralyses truly reforming religious action. We prefer maintenance to prophecy; charity to justice. He lays great stress on the power of imagination at the heart of the Jewish prophetic tradition. Imaginative living shares in God's own imaginative action on behalf of suffering humanity. Postmodern society kidnaps our souls and imaginations through the power of its technology and media. Christian imaginative activity will always want to break out of such confinement. If any kind of spiritual change is going to happen, this is essential. Breuggemann claims that:

> **The task of prophetic ministry is to nurture, nourish and evoke a consciousness and perception alternative to the consciousness and the perception of the dominant culture around us.**[22]

For Breuggemann, this calls not so much for protest against specific issues, although this might be required at times, but for a more general critique of the dominant consensus, that domesticates the alternative vision. To this extent, the prophetic task allies itself with the postmodern agenda of deconstruction. The dominant consciousness has to be criticised and denounced. At the same time, a biblical spirituality and religion cannot just be involved in denunciation, but must engage in the much more difficult task of renewal and reconstruction, not just of our individual lives but also of society. In reviving the biblical tradition of justice for the poor and excluded, Breuggemann would strongly reject much of the postmodern view of spirituality as a personal, private choice.

How can religious believers navigate through the troubled waters of the religion/spirituality debate? While religion appears to be in serious decline in our western world, spirituality continues to fascinate and attract postmodern men and women, especially the young. There has always been tension between the institutional *form* of religion, its structures, laws and practices, and the *spirit*, which seems to express its heart and soul. When a culture is creatively healthy, we find these two elements usually working in harmony, although an institution always seeks to control and corral what it sees as the wider excesses of spirit. When culture is experiencing the kind of profound and rapid change such as today, then the tensions reach breaking point. Vatican II bravely shifted the emphasis away from the Church as institution and hierarchy to the Church as People of God. For a time liberals seemed to be given freedom to live in a much more democratic and less clerical Church

---

22 Walter Breuggemann *The Prophetic Imagination* (Fortress Press Minneapolis 2001) p 3

willing to experiment and respond creatively to the signs of the times. I think it is fair to say that the institutional Church has recently tried to rein in such experiments and creativity. The papacy of John Paul II and Benedict XVI, who worked closely with him in the Holy Office, have both sought to restore ecclesiastical and, especially, papal authority. This has had varying results and it was often remarked how large crowds of young people would gather around Pope John Paul II, who enjoyed almost pop-star status, and yet the same cheering crowds would happily ignore much of his teaching, especially in the area of sexuality. Many young people express love and affection for their parents, but choose to live in a different way.

The attraction of spirituality is that it offers the individual the kind of freedom of choice that the market-driven consumer society is offering. As we have seen, the only Master Story that postmodernism accepts is the story of the Market: as long as you have money and spending power you create your own story. This Master Story is built on power, prestige and possessions. It is the story of the false self, laid bare but now raised almost to the level of a new religion. On any given Sunday morning, you can see lines of *worshippers* heading for the giant shopping-malls that have replaced places of worship. As Christmas draws near this new consumer religion reaches its high point of activity, even frenzy. The mantra is *I shop, therefore I am*. The more I can shop and buy, the more I can distinguish myself and my identity from those who can't. Even spirituality has been co-opted into the life-style pages of the Sunday supplements and the magazines. The shadow-side of this master narrative of the Market – rarely acknowledged – is that it closes off the possibility of a future for the poor.

Whatever criticisms we can make of religion, at its best it always kept alive the memory of the oppressed, the poor, and the excluded. Many spiritual seekers today wish to reject the formal side of the search, the fact that all religions provide boundaries, traditions, rituals, and doctrines. Without any kind of framework the searcher is in dangerous territory and can easily be deluded. Healthy spirituality is always about seeing rightly, and none of us have perfect 20/20 vision. We are conflicted beings. Even when we try to live from our true centre, our true selves, we slip back into our old ways. Perhaps the mistake of religion was to suggest that we could attain the spirituality of perfection. We owned the light but not the shadow and the Church is now paying the price for this in the fall-out surrounding the sexual abuse crisis. At its best, religion reminds us of the need for rituals that teach us not that we are better than others, but that we are in constant need for forgiveness and healing. This is never going to be a popular message but it is a message that critiques the Master Story of consumer spirituality based on the individualistic claim *you are worth it*. Well, we are worth it, but not because of what we own or buy, but because our identity, as we saw in Chapter I, is a given; it is beyond any sense of achievement and worthiness. More to the point, it is an inclusive not an exclusive identity. It not only includes the poor and the rejected, it actually demands a recognition, not a rejection, of the intrinsic poverty that all human beings share before God.

Religion has traditionally offered a package to the next generation, famously expressed in the catechism that supplied answers to all known religious questions. This produced the mentality that we Catholics *had the truth*. There was little recognition of the historical context in which our catechism answers had emerged. After Vatican II, theologians recovered a more authentic view of tradition that sees it not as wholly dependent upon, but in relation to its historical context. For a tradition to survive, as Lieven Boeve maintains, it has to go on re-inventing itself and responding to the new challenges of the age. It cannot just do this by handing on teaching as a kind of package, however updated that might be. It has to reach out in genuine dialogue. Vatican II proclaimed the dignity of the human person at the heart of its theology. Today we see this dignity expressed, not so much through conformity to an unchanging package of truths, as to the very fact of pluralism. The dignity of the person, made in the image and likeness of the divine, always confronts us with what can be called *the irreducible other*.

We have to find ways of putting the bigger picture of the Church in contact with the smaller picture of the individual. *Our Story* needs to be in dialogue with *My Story*. This is the place where true and creative dialogue can happen. No single package of truths can ever define God fully and adequately. God is always surprising us and calling us forth to new journeys. There is a clear pattern in the Bible when God is constantly interrupting the comfort zones of his people. He calls Abraham away from his familiar world. He promises that he and his wife, both well beyond childbearing age, will produce a son. Abraham is then told to sacrifice this very son; when the son is saved, Abraham is told he is to become the father of many people. Throughout the Jewish scriptures, God called unlikely people into leadership. Moses is a law-breaker, even a murderer. David, the least of the brothers, becomes the king. With women, it is almost always a barren women, like Sarah or Hannah, who brings new life, culminating in the young virgin, Mary, who brings forth the Holy One of God.

In Jesus we see the ultimate breaker of religious comfort zones. He constantly challenges the closed narrative that the Jewish Law had become. The poor, the foreigner, the sinner, women, the stranger, the leper, all were excluded to varying degrees from access to God. The very architecture of the Temple in Jerusalem, with its numerous courtyards was a visual testimony to an exclusivist God. Jesus completely rejected that view of God and came into direct conflict with the Jewish religious authorities, a conflict which led to his complete rejection and humiliating death. This death was fully supported by both religious and political authority and took place outside the city walls. It is precisely that rejection that the Father overturns in raising Jesus from the dead. The work of God is to keep all narratives open to the mystery of new life and transformation. The whole ministry of Jesus takes place in this context of openness to the other.

Jesus had an extraordinary ability to listen to and honour the story of each individual he met. He empowered people by placing these stories within the context of his story, *The Kingdom of God*, the bigger picture. The story of the Kingdom took the lives of those who were poor, those who were meek and merciful and those who experienced pain, distress and rejection and declared them blessed. He offered forgiveness and mercy to those who were sinners. At the same time, he challenged them to live more authentic lives, to discover their true selves. The woman taken in adultery was forgiven, her dignity restored, but she was challenged to sin no more. Jesus was opening up the closed narrative of sin/judgement/punishment of her accusers by his challenge to the person in the crowd who was free of all sin to throw the first stone. The role of Jesus is not to condemn but to save. In the famous parable of the Good Samaritan, we see Jesus breaking open the barriers between Jews and Samaritans and in his conversation with the Samaritan woman at the well. In the parable of the Good Samaritan, we see Jesus criticising the priest and the Levite who preferred to keep religious purity laws – after all, they were on their way to the temple – rather than act with compassion. At the well, Jesus listens to the colourful past of the Samaritan woman and turns her into an evangeliser. In his public ministry he is constantly described as being on the move, on the road, moving beyond the physical boundaries of Israel to meet and embrace those beyond.

Jesus was constantly seeking to touch and awaken the true identity of those who felt excluded from God, to reveal that all were sons and daughters of God. Perhaps the most extraordinary illustration of this is his comment at the end of the Sermon on the Mount when he reveals the true purpose of the law as compassion and love for all:

> **You have heard that it was said, 'you shall love your neighbour and hate your enemy.' But I say to you, love your enemies and pray for those who persecute you, so that you may be children of your Father in heaven; for he makes his sun to rise on the evil and on the good, and sends his rain on the righteous and on the unrighteous. For if you love those who love you what**

reward do you have? Do not even the tax-collectors do the same? And if you greet only your brothers and sisters, what more are you doing than others?
Matthew 5

Here we see Jesus opening up the small Jewish narrative to embrace a God who excludes nobody, not even the bad. Looking at the gospels, it is no accident that the hero/heroine of every story is from outside the Jewish system of worthiness. Judaism is archetypal religion. Like every other religion it demonstrates this deep-seated need to separate the worthy from the non-worthy, the pure from the impure, and Jesus always finds God among the impure. Jesus reforms all religion.

A renewed spirituality for today has to link with the dangerous and often unpopular prophetic memory of healthy religion. The story of believers, Our Story, has to include the story of the rejected ones, of those that the market-culture views as of no account. As David Tacey observes:

Religion is rejected not because a person does not believe, but because he or she is not believed. If religion expanded its horizons to include the spirituality of individuals, it might be renewed by such expansion, and individuals would not feel excluded, pushed out or irrelevant.[23]

The shift to personal, inward experience is the great challenge to the old form of religion. As indicated in the last chapter we are no longer served well by paternalistic leadership. The power that Jesus modelled in the gospels was inclusive and non-dominative, servant leadership. It addressed individuals in the reality of their situation. At the same time, he connected the individual to the wider community, the bigger picture, the true self. Individual experience always needs the collected wisdom of the larger group. There is really no such thing as an autonomous Christian. At moments of real distress, such as the death of a loved one, all of us recognise the need to come together in shared ritual. The biblical prophets would have little time for the market idea of the spirit as a personal lifestyle possession.

What religion needs to recognise is that spirit can never be contained and restricted. At the heart of the disillusionment with so much contemporary religion is the sense that it seeks to control and restrict God. Our God has become too small. At this stage in history, we are no longer spiritual children

---

23 David Tacey *The Spirituality Revolution* (Brunner-Routledge 2004) p 37

whose every thought and experience has to be ratified by higher authority. On Mount Tabor the clothes of Jesus are described as dazzlingly white; the apostles are lost for words. No human words can ever describe the mystery of God. The spirit is wild, portrayed in wind and fire at Pentecost, and it is to that wider sense of mystery and search that many are attracted today. We are rediscovering that religion is not primarily a doctrinal matter or moral matter – important though these are – but a mystical one. Today the mystical and the prophetic have to become one. Far from losing religion, this development will help to find its soul.

Chapter 6 – Prayer as Presence

There comes a moment when there arises in your soul a movement that you are at a loss to describe. It moves you to desire you know not what, only that it is beyond your imagining. It is God at work within you.[24]

The debate between religion and spirituality today can be divided into pessimists and optimists. The defenders of traditional religion are the pessimists as they observe the shrinking numbers of practising faithful in the pews, the shortage of vocations, the amalgamating and even closure of parish churches and schools. The optimists all seem to be in the spirituality camp as they see a growing interest in the sense of mystery at the heart of human experience, of the sacred, of the invisible and the intangible which lies both within and beyond our everyday lives. If the Churches are not seen to be feeding my sense of the sacred, I will seek it within. Even scientists today are recognising that there are aspects of human experience that cannot be subject to objective analysis alone. The subjective dimension cannot be ruled out. Experiments are always affected by the observer. What this does is to bring human experience to the fore in a new way.

An adult spirituality is comfortable with mystery and paradox. It recognises the limits of reason; it knows that it doesn't need to know. It teaches the wisdom that I no longer have to be perfect, to solve every problem, to work everything out. It leads me beyond the black and white certainties of the false self that is so quick to analyse and to judge others. It takes me to a place where I discover a deeper kind of knowing. I learn that my life is not about me and the agenda of my small ego, but that I am about life and I learn to live from a new centre. I now see things from a different perspective. I have a new heart, a new way of living. I can now live for God rather than from the social self which I have constructed in response to the expectations of others. This enables me to live the values of the gospel, to work for peace and reconciliation, to reach out to the stranger, to seek to overcome divisions, to learn to live in love. Being human, we slip back into the old ways of the false self, so God has given us a means to stay in the true self. It is called prayer.

The Church has always taught us to pray, but I think that this teaching has concentrated on a prayer agenda for the first half of life. We were taught to *say our prayers*. Nothing wrong with this, but if all we do is *say our prayers* we are neglecting an area of buried treasure in the history of spirituality. This buried

---

24 *The Cloud of Unknowing* Anon

treasure is silent or wordless prayer. It includes what has been described as meditation or contemplation. Meditation, strictly so-called, involves some discursive thinking and imaginative reflection on the mystery of God, or some incident in the life of Jesus. It is a step on the way to contemplation. Unfortunately, the Church has tended to restrict contemplation to a kind of religious elite, such as cloistered monks and nuns. Thankfully, in recent years, there has been a rediscovery that this gift is for everyone. I would suggest that if you are reading this book, some kind of transformative journey has already begun within you. This journey is not of your own making. It is the work of the Spirit.

For some years now, I have had a recurring dream. I am on a journey and have to get from A to B, usually it is a case of getting home. It doesn't matter whether I am travelling by car, train or plane, I never get there. If I am driving, I lose my way; trains and planes invariably are cancelled. Even maps don't seem to make any sense. My frustration level increases until I wake up. This dream could be related to the fact that I travel, often long distances, and it may be expressing a root-fear of not getting to where I should be. The fact that I am usually trying to get home would seem to indicate something else. I think the dream may be expressing a deeper desire. We often speak of the spiritual journey as finding our way home. I recall walking the labyrinth in Grace Cathedral, San Francisco a few years ago. The message that came from the depth of my being having walked reflectively and slowly into the centre of the labyrinth that day was *Take me home*. I have often thought about this sense of *being lost* at the heart of the recurring dream, about not being able to find my way home. I think this is pointing to the fact that we human beings cannot find our way back to God. We cannot resolve the issues of transformation. When we search for God, we slowly become aware that he has already found us: that we are, in fact, already at home. Prayer is becoming present to the God within.

The great paradox of the spiritual quest is that we already have what we are looking for. God is always present to us. Every breath we take each day, every heartbeat, is testimony to God breathing life into us, sharing life with us, calling us into union. All of us are called to intimacy with God. In the Garden of Eden, God walked and conversed with Adam and Eve in the cool of the evening. This is our birthright. It is why God created us. This is the great adventure that often lies buried in our hearts and souls. Sometimes it is never awakened and we live our lives without ever knowing who we are in God. The great mystery of love and communion is lost to us. The spiritual life, therefore, is the call to awaken, discover and live this deepest dream. For long centuries, Christian theology has emphasised the transcendence of God, stressing the fact that God is beyond, located in a distant place called *Heaven*. This is true, but it only tells half the story. In recent years many people are rediscovering the truth that God is also within, that he dwells in our hearts, in the very centre of our being.

But if God has already found us and is dwelling within the very centre of our being why is it that we too often forget that fact? Why is it that we drift back into living as if God isn't really concerned about us? Here we meet the human condition head on. There is no easy way of becoming transformed. No easy way to love and follow a God who does not take us out of life's difficulties and humiliations. Charles Ringma expresses this well when he reminds us that God prefers mystery to magic:

> **The journey towards a mature faith involves a willingness to embrace God for who he is rather than what we would like God to be. It is a bowing before his sovereignty and mystery. And it involves a willingness to embrace the way of God in this world, which is not the way of grandiose power but the way of vulnerable humility.**[25]

Whenever we embark on the spiritual journey, we always encounter in some form or other the Paschal Mystery of Jesus. This is the pattern of death and life, which is at the heart not just of Christian experience but of all human experience. For new life to grow, something has to die. This is experienced most deeply in the spiritual life by the death of that ego-centred existence that is the false self. The issue is always one of giving up control and surrendering to The Great Mystery, The Great Love, The Great River of Life, which Jesus calls *The Kingdom of God*, the experience of deep love and communion. When we are working for others, or even saying our prayers, we are still to some extent in control. In silent prayer, we have to face up to an encounter with our wounded and broken selves. This is why many give up this difficult path. As Jesus said in the parable of the *Sower*, the seed falls among the thorns and stony ground of our human condition.

The biggest obstacle to remaining faithful to silent and wordless prayer is our *thinking,* what has been called our *fly-paper mind.* Thinking is not bad, but it cannot lead us to the true self. When we are thinking we remain in control. We analyse and we judge, usually negatively. Our thinking can only really move us in two directions: the past or the future. What happens when I sit in prayer is that my mind races with thoughts and emotions. I look back at things that have happened in the past. I think of some incident where I have been hurt,

---

25   Charles R Ringma *Hear the Heart Beat* (SPCK London 2006) p 36

of some critical comments I might have received, some negative judgement. My mind flips forward to the future, to some meeting I have to attend, or some difficult person I may want to avoid. All these emotions and thoughts control my mind. All the great mystics tell us that the most difficult place to be present in is the *now*. The now is the place where God is loving me and accepting me with unconditional love. The present moment is the place where I meet a totally non-blaming God.

So how do we learn to deal with all these distracting thoughts and feelings and learn to be present to the now? The key thing is not to get angry and upset with ourselves when we find our minds distracted by thoughts and emotions. They are not bad in themselves, they are not the real you. They are not the deeper life that we have been talking about as our destiny and our deepest reality. So when the distractions come, we have to learn not to judge them, but to observe them with great compassion. We learn to look at them and to let them go. This needs to be done with great gentleness, as St Francis of Sales reminds us, and not with oppositional energy. Fighting them with oppositional energy simply gives them a longer life. Just let them go and say, *That is not me, I don't need this*. Gradually this becomes easier to do, but we will never gain full mastery of this process. To do so would simply let the religious ego back in control: *See how well I am doing, I'm really getting this prayer life under control*. We can never control the spirit of God.

On a recent visit to London, I went to see a collection of paintings by the German artist Hans Holbein, who spent two spells working in England from 1526-28 and 1532-43. He is particularly famous as a portrait painter of prominent figures of the day such as Henry VIII, Thomas More, Erasmus and Jane Seymour. The portraits are stunning in their realism but what struck me was a painting entitled *Noli Me Tangere*. These are the well-known words of the newly risen Christ to Mary Magdalene on the first Easter morning: *Do not touch me, do not cling to me.* In the painting, Mary is reaching out to touch the Lord whom she loves dearly. Jesus holds back, hands raised, to stop this clinging. We always want to cling on to the God we know. During his earthly lifetime, Jesus was constantly reaching out and touching people. Now in his risen life he is indicating a different kind of presence to us. *A presence that will also involve absence.* He gives us his Spirit so that this new kind of presence will lead us to a new and deeper level of communion. Nowhere does this happen more than in prayer. The artist also uses light in an interesting way. Behind Mary Magdalene, two angels can be seen sitting in the tomb, bathed in a quite brilliant light. In contrast, the earthy sky is patchy with the light of early dawn and streaks of cloud. You get a real contrast between the angelic light from the tomb, and the more subdued light of the sky. Our earthly pilgrimage is not an angelic one; that kind of light is too bright for us. Our faith journey has to include both light and dark.

When we begin wordless prayer we may get all sorts of nice warm feelings. God is calling us to a new relationship. These feelings are unlikely to last as we are led to new levels of love. Some purification is necessary here. Our deep-lying wounds and feelings of past rejections may come to the surface. God will carry these for us. We have to acknowledge them, maybe weep over them and know that it is precisely this very woundedness that attracts God to us, just as we saw Jesus reaching out and healing the sick and the suffering of his day; we may experience a kind of nothingness. This is also humiliating for the ego. We are so used to fixing problems and getting results in our calculative minds that we find this difficult. The contemplative mind just learns to look rather than to judge and analyse. A contemplative mind teaches us how to see, to see what is, and look at it with deep compassion instead of judgement.

At the beginning of his ministry we are told that Jesus was led by the Spirit into the wilderness. Mark's gospel expresses this moment very dramatically:

The Spirit immediately drove him out into the wilderness. He was in the wilderness for forty days, tempted by Satan; and he was with the wild beasts; and the angels waited on him. *Mark 1*

The order is interesting. He is first described as being with the wild beasts, only then did the angels minister to him. As in the whole Paschal journey, Jesus always travels first and shows us the way. We needn't be too afraid of the agenda that silent prayer throws up. In therapy, people offload their problems onto a sympathetic listener. God has given all of us the therapy of prayer when we can offload our woundedness onto a loving and compassionate God. We live in a very active and busy culture and a culture that likes to solve problems and fix things. In prayer, we have to move to a very different level. In an earlier chapter, I mentioned how God's love is present to us in crucified form. Even with the best will in the world, we still fall back into unkind judgements of others and other kinds of human weakness. Consistent prayer can help us to move more easily from the narrow ego-agenda of the false self. But we never get it all together. We have to learn to love and accept that we are human. Even though God may be slowly transforming us and purifying us with his love: we are never in control. We cannot engineer this process by our will power – that would be a dangerous victory for the ego. We cannot cling to a God, shaped to respond to the needs of our agenda.

The Spirit of Jesus calls us to this challenging journey in which we learn to become present both to the God within and the God without, the God we learn to see in all people. This kind of presence is difficult. We have been brought up to hide and even disown the less pleasant parts of our lives. This is fine for the first half of life, as we try to build our ego identity. We strive to be successful and to achieve things and we do this by over-identifying with one part of ourselves. We all do this. After all, what would be the point of doing what we are poor at, especially when we have to be successful? Here psychology and spirituality differ. Psychology can offer solutions to many of our problems. Many of these solutions are spiritual, as Carl Jung reminded us. We have to make the crucial step of realising that these problems will not go away. We always carry our wounds. The secret is to accept them and to own them. Presence, in a truly spiritual sense, means being present to all aspects of who I am, the good and the bad, the light and the dark.

When we meet strangers, most of us are on our guard. We put on a public face. This is true of so many human encounters. In our families and our communities, it is more difficult to hide the less attractive side of our personalities. I have lived in religious communities where outsiders speak in glowing terms of a certain person. Members of his community might say, *Yes, but try living with him*. I'm sure the same is true in many families: the greater the light, the greater the shadow. That is why friendships are so important. In friendship we can really open up, be ourselves and be accepted. Richard Rohr suggests that such friendships give us a glimpse of how deeply we are loved and accepted by God in prayer:

> **Have you ever been loved well by someone? So well that you feel confident that person will receive you and forgive your worst fault? That's the kind of security the soul receives from God. When the soul lives in that kind of security it is no longer occupied with technique. We can go back and do the rituals, the spiritual disciplines, but we no longer follow them idolatrously. We don't condemn people who don't do it our way. All techniques, rituals and spiritual disciplines are just fingers pointing to the moon.**

> **But the moon is the important thing, not the pointing fingers. We stand in adoration before the moon. We sing Holy, Holy, Holy. We say, 'Yes, yes, it is good.' We are energized by what we see. And our private darkness is no great surprise. Who cares? Who cares where I am on the ladder of perfection? That's an egocentric**

**question. 'Where am I?' 'How holy am I?' become silly
questions. If God can receive me, who am I not to
receive myself – warts and all?**[26]

When we know we are loved in this way, prayer becomes the greatest empowerment. We can let go of the agenda of the false self and know that our true self shares in the very being of God. This is the whole purpose of the Incarnation. In uniting the divine and the human, Jesus invites us to do the same. In the second half of life, we learn to reclaim our lost selves, the parts of our lives that we have rejected and feared. Most of us discover that *shadow* is not what institutional religion has usually identified as sins of the flesh, but is, in fact, failure itself. Our western shadow, if you like, reveals what we most despise: poverty and powerlessness. We fear being ordinary. Our television screens these days are full of programmes in which many people are trying to show that they have the *X-Factor*, that they can survive the *Big Brother* house and become famous, that they are different from the crowd. Talent is good, but in the spiritual journey, we have to learn to do what Jesus deliberately set out to do: to empty himself, to become ordinary.

Our television programmes are clever in the sense that the participants have to receive the accolade of fame from someone else. It might be a selected panel or simply a vote from members of the viewing public. Presence to God in prayer confers the realisation that our identity is a free gift, that it doesn't have to be conferred by good behaviour or correct liturgical performance. What God wants is a willingness on our part to open our hearts and souls to his love, to be present to what is, to hide nothing, to judge nothing, to reject nothing. In Holbein's portrait, Mary Magdalene is still clutching the jar of spices she had brought to anoint the dead body of Jesus. Such spices are now superfluous. It is we followers of Jesus who will be anointed with the Holy Spirit. In the sacrament of baptism the anointing with chrism, which was used to anoint earthly kings and monarchs, is now used to anoint the Christian believer. Here the ordinary is transformed into the extraordinary.

The prayer of presence doesn't originate with us. All we have to do is to join in the flow of love that exists between Father, Son and Spirit. All we need is loving attention. We don't even have to *think holy thoughts*. We are being invited to a deeper level of being. As we move beyond the calculating mind, we discover that God is unknowable. Our knowledge of God in prayer is gained by entering, what that anonymous English mystic of the fourteenth century famously called, *the cloud of unknowing*. Here we learn to live with paradox and mystery, because this kind of *unknowing* leads us to an emptiness which

---

26 Richard Rohr *Everything Belongs* (Crossroad Publishing Co. NY 2003) p 105

allows us to be filled by God. This kind of loving attention goes beyond feelings and emotions. If we can stay faithful to this process, we learn to see properly. All spirituality is about seeing rightly. We learn to see God in the very core of our being and that leads us to see God's image in every person we meet and in all things. That is the contemplative gaze that simply looks at *what is* with immense compassion because that is the way God looks at everything.

The Cistercian monk, Thomas Keating, has done so much to popularise and open up this kind of wordless prayer for all Christians. He calls it *Centering Prayer* and suggests we try to find twenty minutes or so each day if possible, to be present to God with loving attention. He asks an important question:

Will we ever come to the point where the false self and all the junk is emptied out? I think this is possible, but that does not mean that the results will be what we expected. On the contrary the very capacity to love without self-interest is going to increase our capacity for suffering. The journey, or process itself, is what Jesus called the Kingdom of God. This is a very important point. To accept our illness and whatever damage was done to us in life by people or circumstances is to participate in the cross of Christ and in our own redemption. In other words the acceptance of our wounds is not only the beginning but the journey itself. It does not matter if we do not finish it. If we are on the journey we are in the kingdom. This seems to be what Jesus is saying in the parables. It is in bearing our weakness with compassion, with patience, and without expecting all our ills to go away that we function best in a kingdom where the insignificant, the outcasts, and everyday life are the basic coordinates. The kingdom is in our midst.[27]

When we are brave enough to embrace our humanity and offer it to God, we find ourselves in a realised oneness with God. We are at home in God. We rest in the God who delights in our company. Our task is simply to receive this gift; our active role is to let go of our thoughts and feelings and attend lovingly to the God within. There is no special technique for this, although some teachers suggest the use of a word such as *love*, of Jesus, of the Holy Spirit, to help restore that loving attention when we find our minds seeking to re-assert themselves.

---

27   Thomas Keating *Intimacy with God* (Crossroad Publishing Company NY 20001) pp 90-91

This is where the two journeys of the spiritual life become one, the journey within and the journey without. The more we create space and time for God, the more our hearts are attuned to the suffering of our brothers and sisters, especially the poor, the outsiders, the rejected ones. Once we have had the courage to bring all that we are to the loving and compassionate gaze of God, we can then show our compassionate gaze to those in need. We share a solidarity in poverty and need. Love received always becomes love to be shared. We learn to pray unceasingly as prayer becomes our very breath and energy, our presence to God and to his world. All we have to do is say *Yes* to the great flow within.

When Thomas Merton entered the Trappist monastery of Gethsemane in 1941, he thought he had to show his love for God by despising the world he had left behind. After years of purifying prayer, he learned to accept all of himself, good and bad. In his famous Louisville vision on the corner of Fourth Street and Walnut Street, God showed him the true heart and centre at the core of everyone:

> **It was as if I suddenly saw the secret beauty of their hearts, the depth of their hearts where neither sin, nor desire, nor self-knowledge can reach, the core of their reality, the person each one is in God's eyes. If only they could all see themselves as they really are. If only we could see each other that way all the time. There would be no more war, no more hatred, no more cruelty, no more greed.**[28]

Merton said that he had no special technique for reaching this awareness. What he had learned from long years of prayer was that the Gate of Heaven is everywhere.

---

28 Merton *Conjectures of a Guilty Bystander* (Image Books, Doubleday & Co 1968) p 142

Chapter 7 — God as Mother

In the evolving Mystical Age, humanity will recover the sacred view, which will be not only our salvation but also our freedom and joy. We will be renewed and gifted anew with a sacred view of life when we have confronted our Mystery and penetrated our Deep and discovered the Divine Mother once again, Hagia Sophia, the Sacred Feminine.[29]

If religion and spirituality are to find a fruitful relationship in a postmodern world there needs to be less fear of and more acceptance of diversity and plurality. We need to lose our exclusive ideas and embrace a more inclusive view. This doesn't mean giving up the core of our traditions, but it does call for more flexibility in seeing the essential human dimension in all stories. At the heart of this inclusiveness are our ideas and images of God. The attraction of spirituality today includes a new appreciation of beauty, of art and the imagination, of poetry and deeper appreciation that we walk on sacred ground, in the presence of the divine. This presence permeates our very being and is accessed in prayer. At the same time, we discover what can only be called a darker side of God. Life is not always easy; there are instances of appalling suffering, unjust suffering. Believers have to confront both the light and the dark side of the spiritual task. Not many are prepared to walk this narrow path. Long before religions emerged in the story of humanity, ancient peoples discerned the great pattern of death and life, what we call the Paschal Mystery, in the rhythms of nature. Everything is dying, everything is being transformed and everything belongs. As we say at Mass, *Christ has died, Christ is risen, Christ will come again.*

Central to this recovery of the sacred is the need to explore our images and words about God. God is the ultimate combination of what we mean by our words *male* and *female*. If we are to take women's experience seriously, we have to find ways of naming and honouring the maternal face of God. This has been a major contribution by feminist theologians in recent years. We are losing a small male image of God and learning to find a bigger male and female understanding. This will help us to leave behind the rather rigid, legalist and doctrinal straitjacket that has largely restricted, to our heads, our public discourse and worship. We will learn to move with greater confidence into the spaciousness and beauty of our hearts and souls. Here again personal experience is so important and here we will discover that the mystics have

---

29   Frank X Tuoti *The Dawn of the Mystical Age* (Crossroad Publishing NY 1997) p 68

already gone before us. We will learn how to re-enchant our world and save it from the bleak vision of the one-eyed secularist.

We also need to recover a new and more wholesome way of seeing our world and God's presence in it. For too long we have looked with a divided consciousness which views the world as a kind of cosmic machine made up of many disconnected parts. While we cling to our own private stories and our group stories, we find it hard to reach beyond them to embrace the bigger pattern, the truly human story, which includes everything and sees everyone as touched by the divine. Our faith traditions tell us that we are all made in the image and likeness of God, but we try to control and limit God's presence to our own side. Religion can become very possessive of God. In the gospels, we see Jesus constantly trying to break open the restricted vision and systems of the Jewish leaders. This is not peculiar to Judaism; all religions try to put a stamp of ownership on God. This is the false self, emerging yet again with the all too human desire to control God, rather than let God be free. It has often been said that God created us in his own image and we spend the rest of our days trying to create God in our all too human image. One of the ways in which the Christian Church has tried to restrict our vision of God has been to speak of God in purely masculine language.

For all kinds of reasons, we have chosen to see God through masculine eyes. I think this is one of the crucial reasons why many people, especially women, but not exclusively so, are rejecting religion with its overly rationalistic, moralistic and dogmatic view of God. Some years ago, Robert Sperry discovered that the human brain is bi-cameral. It has a left and right hemisphere. Our western civilisation is almost exclusively left-brain. The left brain is rational, logical and analytic; it has achieved extraordinary things in the area of science and technology, benefits that all of us take for granted. However, there has been a severe price for all this progress: we have neglected the right brain, which is intuitive and artistic. Where the left brain makes distinctions, the right brain seeks connections. Where the left brain seeks rational explanations, the right brain is at home with mystery, paradox and ambiguity. Fortunately, great artists have kept the gifts of the right brain before us. In the area of religion and spirituality, it is the mystics who have spoken the language of the right brain. This is the feminine gift; this is where the Sacred Feminine speaks to us. I am absolutely convinced that it is the Wisdom of the Sacred Feminine, which is behind the great search for spiritual meaning in our world today. Formal religion needs to understand this and react to it to prevent a radical split between religion and spirituality.

I have been arguing in this book that at the heart of all true and authentic religion and spirituality is some inner experience of God's unconditional love for us. For the vast majority of people this is something we gain from a woman rather than a man. This is where the veil first parts and we begin to see what really is. We discover a place of intimacy, of trust, of safety. It is the Great Mystery that all human searching leads to. Instead of *looking for something,* we are *looked at,* instead of *searching,* we are *found* in the deepest and most profound way. This is an experience of God. In recent years, I have preached retreats in many parts of the western world and, sadly, I meet many good people, even hard-working priests and religious, who have what can only be described as a toxic image of God. This would also be true of many who are deserting religion today. If I shared their image of God, I would probably walk away with them.

When we look at the Bible, it seems to be the case that God is looking for images, people who will reflect his likeness, I am using the masculine pronoun here for ease of argument. Right at the beginning of Genesis, we read how God creates both men and women to reflect his image.

So God created humankind in his image, in the image of God he created them; male and female he created them. *Genesis 1*

Now we know that God is beyond gender but in the Bible, it seems that God is always looking for images and likenesses. These are masculine and feminine. We can say that God includes all that we can comprehend as masculine and feminine. Sadly, so much of our discussion of this issue has degenerated into superiority and inferiority. In our history, it is obvious which *side* has won the argument. Even the discussion about language is framed as to which third person pronoun is to be preferred. We Catholics had an advantage, however, in the person of Mary, the one in whom we could glimpse the feminine face of God. Carl Jung, who wasn't a Catholic, said that the declaration that Mary, assumed body and soul into heaven, was the most significant statement of the twentieth century because it placed the feminine firmly in heaven.

The mystics fully understand this. Their preferred word for God is neither *he* nor *she* but *you.* They long to be addressed in the second person. Most languages in the world have two words for *you.* They have an ordinary everyday use and a special word that expresses both intimacy and love, and a sense of special reverence. In English, we don't have this usage, which is probably why we have hung on to the word *thou* in prayer language. Mystics and saints use the word *you* in their communication with God. It is the language of love and tenderness and, at the same time, carries a sense of awe. Martin Buber called it the *I-Thou* relationship. It is special and it is intimate. It communicates that foundational sense that I am beloved of God, as we saw in the first chapter of this book. This is the language of the true self, the language of union.

I think it is beyond argument that this kind of intimate language has come to most of us through our mothers rather than our fathers. However, if it only comes through the feminine then we are left with one of the most deep-seated problems of our time. So many males in our culture suffer what can only be described as the *father wound*. We see this in so many aggressive males who simply don't know how to deal with their anger and sadness. They don't know how to relate to women, how to control their anger, and become addicted to alcohol, or to violence, or simply a kind of numbness of feeling that shuts down much of the joy and creativity of life. Most people seem to have inherited a masculine image of God viewed as an *Old Man in the sky,* who is constantly checking up on our behaviour, more like a disciplinarian, or the *great policeman in the sky,* than a lover.

A few months ago, I was in San Francisco preaching retreats to my fellow Salesians of the western province. One Sunday I wandered into the Catholic cathedral of St Mary's where Mass was just finishing. In most churches in the world, you find people move out quickly at the end of the service, often when the final hymn begins. In St Mary's Cathedral, a large body of the congregation went straight across to the side altar of Our Lady of Guadeloupe. They sang more hymns, accompanied by enthusiastic shouts of *Vivas* as they expressed their affection for the dark virgin of Guadeloupe. The story of this devotion tells us so much about images. Apparently, when the Franciscan missionaries went to evangelise Mexico in 1521 they didn't have much success with the indigenous people. Then in 1531, the dark and pregnant virgin appeared to Juan Diego. The Franciscans took this image around with them and found a much readier response. This was a people who could not read or write, but were so open to the right brain use of images. There have been many claims of appearances of the virgin in recent years, not all may be genuine, but if you visit a place like Lourdes, you can sense the atmosphere at the grotto where Our Lady appeared to the young peasant girl, Bernadette. The famous statue stands in the corner of the grotto in the cleft of a rock, which is womb-like in its appearance. These images of the virgin are so powerful because they show us the feminine face of God. People are deeply attracted to the feminine, as a place of trust. They can believe that a woman, a mother, will always love and accept them. I once listened to a Jesuit theologian from Rome explain how the first experience we have of salvation is when a mother picks up her crying child and says, *It's alright: you are being held.*

Looking back at the twentieth century, we can list many great scientific and technological achievements. History will also look back on this time as the moment in human consciousness when we started to take the feminine mind seriously. It is a different mind and it has never been the dominant consciousness, apart from the mystics and certainly the case of Jesus. Jesus was a man with a profoundly feminine soul. He was kind, nurturing, accepting and compassionate. He clearly had power, as so many of his hearers remarked, but it was a non-dominative power. He wasn't interested in defending boundaries, so much as going beyond boundaries. He acted differently from the usual male pattern. Richard Rohr describes this as the divine breakthrough into human history. The most extraordinary event in the gospels is the Resurrection of Jesus. The first witness is a woman in a culture where no woman could give evidence in a court of law. Even the twelve struggled to believe this message. Both Mark and Luke make it clear that the apostles dismissed the story as, in Luke's words, *an idle tale*.

> **The gospel is a portent of what really was to happen; we would have a hard time with a feminine face for God, a God of ordinary human contact, a God who is a lover instead of a God who is merely known intellectually. Where did Jesus learn to wash the feet of his apostles? (Jn.13:5) In the previous chapter his own feet are washed by a woman, Mary of Bethany![30]**

In his life, Jesus consistently refused the way of violence, compulsion, domination. Sadly, the Christian Church didn't always respect that in some of its more crude evangelising work.

There is no doubt that Jesus used the word *Father* when speaking of God. I agree again with Richard Rohr when he suggests that Jesus is deliberately using the harder word to get across the foundational fact of God's unconditional love in all circumstances. He is saying that even the word *father* is safe, tender, trustworthy, non-blaming and compassionate. And we know that Jesus preferred the intimate word *Abba* to address God, to the evident consternation of the legalistic and rigid Jewish leaders. I shall say more of God as Father in the next chapter. Healthy spirituality and healthy religion need to find a place for a masculine way of loving and a feminine way of loving. Thankfully, you will find some men who have a well-developed feminine consciousness, and you can also find some women who don't.

In the history of spirituality, men who had a strong feminine consciousness, were dismissed as academic theologians and sidelined as mystics. Some women mystics were not canonised, such as Julian of Norwich, Hildegard

---

30   Richard Rohr *Simplicity* (Crossroad Publishing Company NY 2003) p 28

of Bingen and Mechtild of Magdeburg. I referred earlier to the problem many Christians have today with the Church's teaching in the area of sexuality. I don't think there can be any doubt that throughout Christian history we have generally presented a negative view of the body. Now the mystics don't have this problem. They do not see the body as bad, to be denied or rejected. This positive view of the body did not prevail. Dualism triumphed and the body continues to be seen as needing to be repressed in the spiritual journey. In its extreme form this view led to excessive penances such as the use of the discipline on the body. The ideal Christian pastor had to be seen as a kind of disembodied being who lived beyond all passion and enthusiasms. Women were viewed with suspicion by an all-male clerical Church. A religion that promotes such a negative view of the body is blocking the truth of the Incarnation. A more inclusive view would have taken on board the liberating feminine perspective that the body is good. Today we are beginning to grasp that there is something a woman knows in her body that a man will never know. This refers to the whole area of transformation. Women's bodies are places of transformation through the miracle and mystery of childbirth as a new life is nurtured and fed by the mother's body.

It is no surprise that most churches are dominated by the presence of women. Most religious orders are feminine. It seems that women have an instinctive feel for spirituality. Maybe that is why we men are occupying all the positions of power and organisation. It gives us something to do. We are not as comfortable with transformation, but we do like to run things! What we have to lose in this new twenty-first century is our one-sided view of things. We have to move beyond gender wars to a new kind of mutuality. We have to create a new spiritual marriage between the masculine and the feminine. All great religions have to be about transformation and unless we learn the mystery of transformation we will go on transmitting our pain. We have to learn this together as men and women today.

The issue of losing our religion can be viewed today as a necessary process of growth to a richer and deeper understanding. We are moving from the patriarchal, masculine model of Church, which emphasised the exterior structure, its institutional aspects: hierarchy, obedience, power and control over peoples' lives. We can no longer regard the faithful as obedient, silent followers. We no longer live in a world of *father knows best*. Searchers for God in these difficult postmodern days are looking for a much greater recognition of the feminine face of God. It is not a question of replacing a masculine-dominated religion with a feminine-dominated spirituality. It is a question of getting the balance right. That means a much greater appreciation and awareness of feminine ways of knowing, of learning to live with paradox and ambiguity, of recognising the importance of inner experience in prayer alongside action on behalf of a better world. It is looking for both a religion and a spirituality that recognises boundaries, but can comfortably go beyond them. It seeks connections rather then fragmentation.

This is the gift of the sacred feminine that is coming more and more into the consciousness of spiritual seekers today. Our lost and confused humanity needs a real re-birth by entering into the womb of the sacred feminine. We have to lose the false self with its ego-centred programmes, which are causing so much death and destruction to our fragile planet and our fragile souls. We hear the voice of Nicodemus in our times asking an age-old question:

> **'How can anyone be born after having grown old? Can one enter a second time into the mother's womb and be born?' Jesus answered, 'very truly I tell you, no one can enter the kingdom of God without being born of water and Spirit. What is born of the flesh is flesh, and what is born of the spirit is spirit.'** *John. 3*

Jesus is clearly speaking here about the need for transformation from the false self, the flesh, to the new life of the spirit. Our civilisation, and our understanding of religion, have been long dominated by masculine consciousness. The stress has been on external action, of changing things from above, of fixing and controlling. We have achieved many things but the cost is getting higher. This cost is being paid by our planet and our environment; it is being paid by the poor, and it is being paid in our affluent countries in our widespread relational woundedness. The task today is to integrate masculine and feminine properly and it is taking place in a difficult atmosphere. Our media and culture promote sexual activity on every level; at the same time, we have lost our ability to stay faithful as lovers. We seem to want the pleasure, but we can't handle the pain of relationships. The Church often bemoans the sexual immorality of our age, yet the Church will not be listened to unless we learn how to put masculine and feminine together in a more harmonious and creative way.

At the heart of this re-birth is a new understanding of the mystery of mutuality. It is this mystery that a woman naturally understands especially when she has carried a child within her body. That child will be slowly nurtured into life and birth. It will then exist outside the body of the mother yet forever deeply connected and united. This is the great mystery of the giving and receiving of love and life that we meet in the Trinity. It is the paradox of mutual in-dwelling and is the language of the mystics. We see it mirrored in Mary, the great mother, who gives flesh and blood to her son Jesus. Yet almost every great painting of the Madonna and Child shows Mary holding the child not to her motherly breast, but outwards, away from her body, as a gift to us all. *This is for you.* Mary is always saying *this is for you*, which is why as he lay dying on the cross Jesus blessed this mystery of motherhood and union as he looked at Mary and John and said, *This is your son. This is your mother.*

There is nothing we can ever do to earn this kind of gift. It is all about mutuality, it is all relational. All of us have been created for this mystery of transformation, whereby we can live in God, and God in us. This was exactly what Jesus spoke about on the night before his death with his still uncomprehending disciples gathered round him at the last supper:

> **I will ask the Father, and he will give you another Advocate, to be with you forever. This is the spirit of truth ... You know him because he abides with you, and he will be in you... ..On that day you will know that I am in the Father and you in me and I in you.** *John 14*

The mystics know this, and yet it is always difficult to put into words. St Catherine of Siena once said, *My deepest me is God.* Some theologians might be shocked by this, but it only echoes the words of Jesus.

The mystics have always been a bit of a threat to the authority of the Church because their authority comes from a deeper place, the very core of their being. They have uncovered the Great Mystery, or rather had it revealed to them. It doesn't depend on documents or theological statements. It is an experience. Once it is experienced it can never be lost. Julian of Norwich speaks with ease and familiarity of Jesus as our mother in whom we are endlessly carried and out of whom we can never come. That is maternal, feminine language. Mary is the great example of this, which is why Catholics always find her such a fascinating figure. She is the human image of transformation. In her body God assumes humanity and Mary is then transformed into God's own life and becomes the great symbol of what should be happening in all our lives.

A mother is characterised by *attentive loving*. She watches her baby grow and change and she has to be attentive to this process. A woman knows this particular child, in this particular situation, at this particular time. Men prefer to define, to categorise and to systematise. Women can deal with complexity, with difference, with ambiguity. She has to guide her child through moments of pain and tears and find a variety of ways to do this. In child-rearing, one size doesn't fit all. Men prefer the dualistic patterns of the good guys and the bad guys, who wins and who loses. We see the tragedy of this in the current disastrous campaign in Iraq where our male political leadership (supported by some women, we have to say) are demanding complete and total victory over their enemies. It was a Hindu, Mahatma Gandhi, who asked us Christians why we never believed the Sermon on the Mount.

Many people today live their lives in fear. Fear of crime, fear of terrorism, fears of human differences, of race, or of religion. Our times face difficult challenges but we have also discovered the gift of feminism in these times. This gift teaches that we must learn to accept and reverence the presence and the complexity of *the other*. We can no longer demand that everybody else must mirror our own culture. We can no longer claim – as we Catholics used to do – that we have all the truth and everybody else has to conform to us. We are not being asked to abandon our own tradition and its story, but it needs to expand in two directions. It needs to learn to listen to and take seriously the particular story and experience of each individual. At the same time it needs to include the common humanity of all. This is the gift of the sacred feminine: to see connection, mutuality and unity in diversity. This takes us into a world of greater complexity, a truly adult world, in which one side doesn't have to be totally right and the other side totally wrong.

A few years ago, I was visiting Durham Cathedral in the north east of England. Behind the main altar, I discovered a most remarkable representation of the Pieta. It was created out of two tree trunks, one horizontal, representing the dead body of Jesus, while the vertical tree represented Mary. The branches were so arranged that the arm of Mary was reaching out to the dead body of her Son. The amazing part of this work of art was that one of the branches representing the arm of the dead body of Jesus was responding to the invitation of Mary. We all know that theologically it is the Father who raised Jesus from the dead. But this artist – a woman – had brilliantly visualised how life comes to us from our mother and this love is stronger than death and this love comes from the heart of God.

Chapter 8 — God as Father

We know that God is neither masculine nor feminine, and we must continue to use feminine images for God, too, but the father wound is so deep and so pervasive in much of the world and in much of history, that even Jesus needed to use the more daring, the more distant and the more dangerous word for God – Abba – because that is where the wound lies for so many.[31]

The search for a deeper and more satisfying spirituality is leading to the discovery and recognition of the feminine face of God. This is one of the most significant signs of spiritual growth in our times. It is not a question of replacing predominantly masculine images of God with feminine ones, but of embracing a much richer and more comprehensive understanding, while acknowledging that our minds can never fully comprehend the mystery of God. We need a *both/and* approach which requires a new look at what we mean when we use masculine images of God. This is vital not just for our personal lives as men, but also for family life and for the regeneration of our postmodern society. Men need to re-think the issue of power. There is plenty of evidence of destructive power in the violence that scars our world today, and also in the relational failures that leave families split and in some cases abandoned. This has serious consequences for all children, but especially for young males, many of whom suffer from what has been called, the *father wound.*

I live, in Bootle, Liverpool, a short distance from the estuary of the River Mersey where it merges into the Irish Sea. I often go there to walk and to pray. In the last 15 months an amazing piece of public art has appeared on the two mile stretch of Crosby Beach in Liverpool Bay. It consists of 100 life-size male statues cast in iron. Its official name is *Another Place* by Antony Gormley; the locals call them the Iron Men of Crosby. In the space of fifteen months, over 600,000 visitors from across the UK and beyond have come to see these statues. It is a tidal beach and some of the statues get submerged while others protrude from the sea. His work has been described as having a real missionary zeal, not completely divorced from his Catholic roots. I must say I love these statues and like all works of art, they touch different levels. Many locals have dressed them up in Liverpool and Everton football hats; they have been decorated with shopping bags from various stores, and even had

31 R Rohr & J Martos *From Wild Man to Wise Man*
    (St Anthony Messenger Press Ohio 2005) p 69

the local newspapers pushed into the arms. Last Christmas a Nativity play took place in and around the statues.

Many people seem drawn to contemplation in this open space of sea and sand, with the mountains of North Wales as a backdrop, and the horizon stretching into the distance. These male bodies stare out into the horizon, reminding us of the rich maritime past of Liverpool as a great seafaring port, much of which has now been lost, and yet looking out into the horizon with a kind of haunting expectancy. In many ways they sum up the theme of this book: what we have lost and what we are still looking for.

For me also they represent much of the anguish and uncertainty of the male soul. There is a sense of loss about many men today, and we are still not quite sure what we are looking for. Certainly many men have abandoned religious practice, but I think that the loss goes deeper. It goes back to the issues raised in the early chapters of this book. It is about identity. We don't know who we are. In our secular western society we are left only with the false self, that ego-centred identity that simply cannot carry the burden and mystery of what it means to be human. The false self is endlessly needy, fragile and very insecure. It is caught in the treadmill of power, prestige and possession. It is not connected to the bigger picture, any sense that a richer and deeper life can be available once we discover the true self. Now this identity problem affects both men and women but it seems to affect men and women in different ways.

The rise of feminine spirituality called into question many aspects of male behaviour that had long been unquestioned. The patriarchal culture of *father knows best* has been seriously dismantled by feminist critique. It had to go, not only because it was undermining women but also because it damages the souls of men. Men (and some women today, especially in western culture) are brought up to compete, to achieve, to be powerful and successful. This is what society rewards. It is all about self-control and controlling the live of others. At the same time, men struggle with relational issues; with the inner journey. When relationships get difficult, men (and some women) walk away.

Robert Johnson argues persuasively that the price of our scientific and technological success is being paid in our wounded-feeling function. The word *feeling* is not the same as emotion. It goes deeper. The feeling function is the capacity to value or to give worth to something. It is what we need to search for; it is the great quest of the soul. In his analysis of the story and myth of the Holy Grail, he puts his finger on the central spiritual issue that all of us face:

> **The meaning of life is not in the quest for one's own power or advancement, but lies in the service of that which is greater than one's self. Carl Jung made this statement in more modern terms when he said that the meaning of life is to relocate the center of gravity of the personality from the ego to the Self. If I asked what is the meaning of life, most people would answer that it is to serve me – my ego plans and involvements. The revelation of the Grail castle is that life serves something greater than one's self.**[32]

Johnson suggests that the shift from *Ego* to *Self* requires a Copernican revolution as painful in our personality as the Copernican revolution was to the pre-modern mind. In using the word *painful,* Johnson gets to the core of the spiritual search. None of us wants to give up control and power. None of us wants to give up the agenda of the ego-centred false self. It feels like dying. Yet it is precisely this issue that all authentic religion leads to. Jesus meets it head on, but he experienced great difficulty in getting his closest male followers to understand it.

What we are discovering today is that long before the great religions appeared in the world there was plenty of received wisdom about growing up and maturing. This wisdom could be found in all cultures, the aboriginals of Australia, the

---

32 Robert A Johnson *The Fisher King and the Handless Maiden*
(Harper Collins San Francisco 1993) p 46

tribes of Africa, the Native American Indians. These ancient peoples knew that young men did not naturally grow up: *they had to be taught.* Therefore, they would be taken away from the female members of the tribe to be led by older men into solitude, or what can only be described as liminal space, so that they could become men. In our sophisticated postmodern world, we see so many men who have not grown up. We can see it in our politics, in the Church, and in our local communities. In the war on terror, we are told that the goal is complete and total victory, and any kind of violence seems justified in pursuing that, even the torture of prisoners. We see a Church that still doesn't know how to share power with women, and many priests who assume autocratic control of their parishes. In local communities, we have young men who drift into violent gangs in order to find some kind of identity and significance for themselves. I was in a Salesian parish just a few weeks ago where the parish priest was burying a young man who had been stabbed to death. He told me that it was the fourth such murder in the area in the last few weeks.

The ancient cultures seem to intuit the fact that the male had to be taught and that the teaching wasn't soft or gentle. It had a certain brutality to it. These men knew that life had a meaning and that meaning was not centred on the ego. They instinctively knew that life was hard and inevitably involved some experience of suffering. They knew that life was short and would end in death and all these facts should shape the way a man had to live. They intuited the great patterns that they saw in nature, the rhythm of dying and changing, and knew that men had to learn to fit their lives into these great patterns, not the other way round. Long before religion became organised on our planet, these ancient cultures knew that men had to be initiated by some kind of sacred ritual into these patterns of transformation.

Women did not seem to need the same kind of initiation because, as we have seen, they learned about the mystery of pain and suffering in their own bodies. Patriarchal culture always placed them in the inferior position, the second place. The Catechism of the Catholic Church teaches that God is beyond male and female, but it is *appropriate* to call him *Father*. That word *appropriate* indicates again the fear of the feminine which is still part of our current Church leadership. Women who undergo menstruation, and labour, and the menopause, know at a very deep corporeal level what men need to be taught. Women who give birth know the price of bringing a new life into this world. It was assumed that women did not need to be taught the language of powerlessness. In western culture, that is no longer the case and some women today need to be taught how to handle power without abusing it.

Men seem to encounter the mystery of blood and suffering in war. It is observed that boys become men very quickly on the battlefield. Most societies respect and honour those who fight for their countries as we see in remembrance ceremonies, but today we seem to be hearing more disturbing stories about soldiers mistreating and torturing prisoners and killing innocent civilians. We also see women today in positions of power who abuse that power.

You could argue that religion has its own sacraments of initiation which have outgrown the need for other rituals. Generally speaking these appeal more to the feminine than the masculine. We dress children up and prettify the whole experience. I'm not against infant baptism, but pouring a little water over the head of a baby in a beautiful flowing gown cannot be compared to the drama of an adult stripping off clothes and being immersed completely in water. Paul is constantly speaking about being baptised into the *death* of Christ and rising to a new life. When I was confirmed I remember the tap on the cheek from the bishop. Even that has gone now. Ancient initiation rites used to strike young boys, even cut them, to wound them to remind them that they had to learn to own their own pain and suffering in life and not inflict it on others. Many used circumcision, and it was precisely when the young boy was experiencing pain that he would be taught by the elders. Too many of our liturgies are wrapped up in lace and flowers and gold and rarely seem to appeal to the wildness of the male soul and spirit. Young people have very few mentors who have walked the great journey into wisdom and compassion; it seems that our traditional religion and its rituals appear to have lost something transformative.

Religion shifted the emphasis from the need for initiation to the importance of the end of life. The whole stress on saving my individual soul was part of this. We had to hope and pray that a priest would be present on our deathbed, or at the scene of an accident. It was all about the next life and making sure of entry. This is religion as insurance policy. There was little, if any, emphasis on transformation *now*, of being aware that eternal life begins in this world; it was all about the last half-hour. Initiation rituals, on the other hand, taught about living life now, understanding that the great pattern of meaning shapes the rest of life. Without that kind of awareness, young men would become cynical, apathetic, or violent. We are made by God for something else, what can only be described as a spiritual journey, which is going to involve some pattern of death and life.

When we consider how Jesus trained his closest followers, he is clearly leading them into an experience of initiation. They must have been very excited when he first sent them out to preach and heal in his name. Consider how he prepares them *for the journey*. He tells them to take nothing with them: no haversack, no food, no money, and no spare clothes (Luke 9). I wonder what they made of that! He seems determined to move them into an initiation experience where they have to rely totally on the providence of God, not their own resources. When a man declared that he would follow Jesus anywhere he is told that he will have nowhere to lay his head (Matthew 8). There is a very dramatic moment when the Pharisees and Scribes approach Jesus and ask him for a sign to prove that he is from God. Jesus gives a quite extraordinary answer:

> **An evil and adulterous generation asks for a sign, but no sign will be given to it except the sign of the prophet Jonah. For just as Jonah was for three days and three nights in the belly of the sea-monster, so for three days and three nights the son of Man will be in the heart of the earth.** *Matthew 12*

Like all the great heroes of mythic literature, Jesus points to a journey, a quest, a search that will encounter strange beasts and monsters. He uses this dramatic and archetypal metaphor to get across the heart of his message: something has to die for new life to emerge, something precious has to be lost. This is the mystery of the great transformation, what the Church calls the Paschal Mystery.

This process of leading them further into this journey of vulnerability reaches its climax in his predictions that his ministry will end in rejection, suffering, failure and death. On every occasion, his closest friends and followers are completely confused. It is often remarked in the debate about women priests that Jesus obviously chose twelve men as his apostles. If it is true that our most intimate and tender experience of God is centred on the feminine dimension of God, then Jesus seems to go out of his way to convince us that God as Father is also a totally safe image of God's unconditional love. Jesus tries to lead his followers through the dark journey of suffering and death. At the heart of authentic religion and spirituality there has to be an encounter with blood and with pain. The death of our ego-centred life is that last death we want to undergo. Men especially, as we have seen, have to be taught this mystery of letting go, of surrender to a Great love, the embrace of God as both Father and Mother.

We shouldn't be surprised at the incomprehension and genuine fear of the disciples of Jesus on hearing this teaching about transformation through suffering. In his gospel, Mark describes three occasions when Jesus makes this journey of descent very clear to his followers (chapters 8-10). At the first instant, Peter takes Jesus aside and rebukes him, immediately after correctly identifying Jesus as the Messiah. Correct knowledge doesn't necessarily lead to conversion. As mentioned earlier, Jesus reacts by calling Peter, *Satan*. On the second occasion, Mark records their reaction very clearly:

They did not understand what he was saying and were afraid to ask him. *Mark 9*

The apostles, like most of us, were on the journey of ascent, not descent. They expected Jesus to triumph as Messiah leaving them to bask in the glory of the various top jobs that would come their way. They react to his second prediction of suffering and rejection by having an argument about which of them was the greatest. With great patience, Jesus takes them aside and tells them that the greatest of them must be the least. Unless they know and experience some kind of powerlessness, to be at the bottom of the pecking order, they will be tempted to abuse power. A third time Jesus tries to lead them into the journey of descent. Mark describes the apostles as being afraid, and in something of a daze. Once again, they miss the point, James and John come up to Jesus to ask him a favour: they want the top places at his right and left hand when he comes into his glory! Jesus tells them that they have to learn to drink the cup of suffering. The other ten apostles are described as being very angry with James and John.

We live in an age of spin-doctors. Our political leaders are surrounded by advisors, who are constantly trying to spin negative stories into positive ones. Not just in politics, as we have seen to our cost in the Church's fumbling attempts to deny the reality of child abuse. Thankfully, the evangelists are not spin-doctors. The many failures of Peter and the other leaders are all laid bare for us to see. After trying to initiate his followers, Jesus then does the journey of descent himself, in his passion and death. In his agony in Gethsemane, he addresses God in his most tender masculine form: as Abba. On the Cross, that loving presence seems to have been withdrawn from him; yet Jesus is able to move from the anguish of, *My God, my God why have you forsaken me?* to the trust and surrender of, *Father, into your hands I commend my spirit.*

We know that we can receive unconditional love from our mothers and our fathers, but masculine love has another dimension to it. It includes a *conditional* element. Our mother's love reflects in a small but vital way the fact that the unconditional love of God is always unearned, a gift, something we can never be worthy of. Our father's love will challenge us, to grow, to move out into the world, to do something significant, to make a difference, to try to make the world a better place. We see Jesus saying, *if you obey the commandments.* Both boys and girls, but especially boys, need to win the approval of their fathers. A pat on the back, an embrace from father to son is a unique and life-enhancing blessing. While our mothers remind us of the mystery of love and union, our mature masculine love will lead us on the journey, into an adventure, into the quest:

The relationship between fathers and sons is too deep for words and touches upon primeval and foundational longing. A son wants Dad to give him his male energy, and then he wants to know that he has something to give back to his father almost as an equal... He does not just want to be on the receiving end. It is the mutual self-giving of father and son which creates Spirit, which is the basic metaphor for God in much of John's gospel.[33]

This need of affirmation and approval is true also for girls, but we are living in an age when there are not too many male figures able to pass on this gift of blessing and acceptance to their children. *Father hunger*, or the *father wound*, may be the greatest experience of poverty in our affluent western world.

Maybe one of the reasons why many are losing their religion today is because we took this daring and life-enhancing journey of Jesus and turned it into a question and answer experience. He invited us to share an adventure and we reduced it to moral niceties. Jesus was trying to situate our lives in the bigger picture, the great mystery that takes suffering and death and transforms it into new life and love; that takes failure and transforms it into victory; that takes anxiety and transforms it into faith and trust. He invites us to shed the protective shell of the false ego-centred self and plunge into the mystery of receiving the gift of God-self, of the mystery of mutuality. It is all about participation in this great mystery that he called *The Kingdom of God*, who loves us like a mother and lovingly challenges us like a father. Our lives take shape beyond the small and insecure self and we learn to be held by the right and the left hand of God. When we know at the deepest level of our being that we are loved unconditionally, we are no longer afraid to face what can only be called the dark side of God. Someone once said that in the first half of life we have to fight the devil. We need to learn self-control and the necessary virtues. We know there are limits and boundaries. In the second half of life, we learn to fight God. This is a much scarier adventure, which is probably why religion spends too much energy in fighting the devil.

Beating the devil can be a huge victory for the ego. Jesus warns of the danger of sweeping the house clean only to find seven more devils have taken control. Fighting God is much more challenging. Not many people want to confront the dark side. We don't know what to do with our pain and our suffering. In the harsh and critical climate of our postmodern world, we are all happy to point out, ridicule and amuse ourselves at the faults of others. In looking at the

---

33 Richard Rohr *Adam's Return* (Crossroad Publishing NY 2004) p 89

weaknesses of others, I can always bask in the glory of my superiority. That is the path of the untransformed hero, who will never bring about any renewal or regeneration.

All heroes have to come to terms with some kind of wound. Jacob is the classic spiritual hero who wrestles all night with the angel and demands a blessing. He wins the blessing but at a price: he walks away wounded at the hip (Gen 32). Jesus teaches that our wounds have to become sacred or they will embitter us. So many angry people today do not know how to deal with their pain or the pain of the world. Much of the rejection of postmodern atheism is rooted in a great disappointment with God. Jesus refuses to become the hero who kills the bad and rewards the good. He doesn't play that game. He demonstrates how to be the victim in an entirely new way, one that seeks reconciliation not rejection. This is how our wounds become sacred. There is no such thing as perfect world, perfect Church, perfect family, perfect community because there are no perfect individuals. Initiation rituals taught young men how to live with the wound of imperfection; how to deal with life, that can be at times hard and unjust; how to live with their imperfect selves. Jesus is the supreme example of this kind of teaching, except that even we Christians failed to realise that we have to undertake the same transforming journey. Without this, we simply go on repeating the agenda of the first half of life. We go to church, we keep the rules of morality and ritual, but there is little sign of transformation. We need spiritual, wounded heroes today.

This demands a Copernican shift from the ego to the self, the realisation that there is a deeper mystery at work in our world; one that I cannot fix or control but to which I must eventually surrender. For this to happen there has to be a great defeat of the ego, some experience of the woundedness of reality. We see so many young men, and women today, who appear lost, unaware of any nobility or greatness about life. They haven't tasted the mystery. They need adults who can lead them there, who can teach them not to be afraid of the dark. All great heroes and heroines go to the place of danger, the dark wood, or the open sea, the place where I reach the end of my resources. These great mythical stories are stories about our souls. We will only be able to lead our young into this place of discovery if we ourselves as adults have made that same journey and emerged with wisdom and compassion, rather than bitterness, cynicism and anger. The masculine face of God draws us into the journey, into the belly of the whale. The feminine face of God welcomes us into a place of union, where diversity is seen as one, where wounds become sacred, and where we begin to taste eternal life in the now. We need both.

Chapter 9 — Learning to see in the dark

They came to Bethsaida. Some people brought a blind man to him. He took the blind man by the hand and led him out of the village; and when he had put saliva on his eyes and laid his hands on him, he asked him, 'Can you see anything?' And the man looked up and said, 'I can see people, but they look like trees, walking.' Then Jesus laid his hands on his eyes again; and he looked intently and his sight was restored, and he saw everything clearly. *Mark 8*

Jesus said to him, 'What do you want me to do for you?' the blind man said to him, 'My teacher, let me see again.' Jesus said to him, 'Go; your faith has made you well.' Immediately he regained his sight and followed him on the way. *Mark 10*

The city of San Francisco has a special charm and beauty. Known locally as the City by the Bay wherever you wander you are drawn to the stunning beauty of the harbour whose entrance is guarded by the magnificent Golden Gate Bridge. In the centre of the bay lies the mysterious presence of Alcatraz. Like so many visitors, I was anxious to visit the famous rock. The experience was memorable, even chilling at times, as you tried to imagine what it was like for inmates to be locked up in those tiny cells. As I listened to the portable CD guide, I was struck by the voice of former prisoners who share some of their memories. A prisoner who broke the rules usually ended up in solitary, in a damp, very cramped space with no light. One prisoner described how he would rip off a small button from his uniform and throw it on the floor. He would crawl around in the dark until he found it. He would do this five or six times, until he began to see in the dark.

We find ourselves living in dark days, times of uncertainty and change. Saints and mystics who make the spiritual journey often speak about the dark night of the soul, a period of real trial and testing. It normally refers to the individual journey. I think that what is happening to religion today can be described as a kind of collective dark night. It affects all religious believers to a greater or lesser extent, from the Church leaders struggling to find new vocations, to parishioners grieving at the closing of a parish church, or the Catholic teacher struggling to keep up numbers in a school. We can all see the ageing of the clergy, the decline of marriages and baptisms, the alienation of the young. At the same time, we see non-believers being very critical of religion and many believers seem lost in a kind of mediocrity. There isn't much passion and fire around, and what there is seems to have been hijacked by radical fundamentalists who spew out a witch's brew of hatred and violence.

It helps if we can see some kind of pattern in these turbulent times. Our culture so often teaches us that in life we are expected to be happy and to solve all our problems. In my many visits to the USA, I am still affronted by the relentless cry of shop assistants and store workers to *have a nice day!* Well, maybe it's my European pessimism, but often enough we don't have nice days. Some might even be disastrous. The point I am making is that we need these moments of darkness and defeat to learn who we really are and to become who we are meant to be. Disappointments and difficulties pare life down to its essentials. They help us to see in a new way. Therapy tends to suggest that all problems can be healed. Spirituality on the other hand, goes deeper and views these experiences as opportunities to move from the control model to a surrender pattern. We begin to see our wounds not so much as imperfections to be healed but as opportunities for soul work. We begin to recognise and honour our complexities. We become artists, creating a more soulful identity.

Have you ever noticed how little time Jesus spends in the officially holy places of his time, and when he did go there he is described as encountering a demon, being rejected, and getting angry and turning over the money tables. In contrast he seems to be constantly on the move, happy to work inside his Jewish boundaries, but equally happy to move beyond them. Take these examples just from Matthew's gospel:

Jesus was led by the spirit into the wilderness. c 4

As he walked by the Sea of Galilee he saw two brothers. c 4

When Jesus saw the crowds, he went up the mountain. c 5

He gave orders to go over to the other side. c 8

He crossed the water and came to his own town. c 9

As Jesus was walking along, he saw a man called Matthew. c 9

As Jesus went on from there two blind men followed him. c 9

Jesus went out of the house and sat by the lake. c 13

Now when Jesus heard all this he withdrew from there in a boat to a deserted place by himself. c 14

Immediately he made the disciples get into the boat and go on ahead to the other side. c 14

They came to land at Gennesarat. c 14

Jesus went away to the district of Tyre and Sidon. c 15

Then he left them and went away. c 16

When Jesus had finished saying these things he left Galilee and went to the region of Judea beyond the Jordan. c 19

While Jesus was going up to Jerusalem, he took the twelve disciples aside by themselves. c 20

The same pattern can be found in the other gospels. Jesus is constantly on the move, he often withdraws from the crowds, he goes off alone or with his disciples. He visits areas beyond Judaism and he is often in a boat crossing the lake. He doesn't restrict his view of the sacred to the holy places. He sees the sacred everywhere. In view of our current cultural and religious climate, I want to reflect a little on two often-neglected aspects of Jesus' ministry and lifestyle: his openness to strangers and foreigners, and his constant journeys over water.

Many classic stories and myths refer to night sea journeys. It is a common and profound metaphor for the life of the soul and the spirit. In the last chapter, I referred to Jesus' use of the Jonah story to describe his own life and its encounter with suffering. In the biblical account, God summons Jonah to accomplish a task. He is to preach to the Ninevites. This is the last thing Jonah wants to do so he escapes on a ship bound for Tarshish. A storm threatens the safety of the crew, and when they discover that Jonah is running away from God, they decide to throw him overboard. He is swallowed by a large sea monster (a whale or large fish) in which he sits for three days and three nights before he is spat out onto land. At that point, God calls him again, and this time he responds.

When Jesus says this is the only sign he will give to prove that he is from God then we need to pay some attention. Water and the sea are always symbols of the unconscious and the image of Jonah sitting in the belly of the sea monster and then thrown out again is an archetypal image of death and rebirth. When we sit in the belly of the beast, we experience a real loss of something precious. The institutional Church today sits in such a dark place. There has been a sharp fall from respect and favour and we are undergoing a kind of death with the daily struggles to close churches, to cluster parishes, to amalgamate others. I can remember when I was first ordained, teaching religious education and working alongside many fellow Salesians in our Catholic high school. Today we have only one member of the order on the staff. Like so many other teaching orders, we are struggling to find ways of handing on the charism (the particular spirit) of the order to lay people. Most schools, formerly run by religious, now have lay leadership. Young people no longer feel inspired to give their lives as priests and religious as was true previously. Last year I addressed a conference of religious working in hospital ministry. Much of the discussion was about long-established religious congregations looking to amalgamate with other like-minded congregations.

This is why I am suggesting that the dark night is being experienced collectively these days, especially in western secular culture. The United States has a much greater church-going population but the vocation pattern is reproducing what is happening in other parts of the western world.

I am trying to suggest that we should not be surprised at these developments. As we saw earlier, Jesus is not a conventional *business as usual* religious teacher. He is a wisdom teacher rather than a manager. He is constantly trying to get us to see more clearly and to look out at the expanding horizon. For his followers this might seem like death. Sitting in the belly of the whale is not a nice place to be. But something profound is happening. We are living through the painful process of death and resurrection. There is some dying of the ego going on here. We cannot deny that at times in religious history, when the Church was successful and powerful, there were real abuses of power happening. Today we are experiencing a real wounding, yet this process is leading us to the very heart of transformation. We are having to learn to stand on our own two feet, to live a mature adult faith, to learn to see in the dark.

It is usually circumstances that create the possibility for change. At the heart of our current troubles, the Spirit of God is moving over the waters as she did at the very outset of the creation story. We are re-discovering the maternal face of God, the compassionate embrace that reaches out to include and not to exclude, that recognises complexity, difference, and ambiguity. In this sense, postmodernism opens up new possibilities for change and transformation. As Sandra Schneiders points out:

> **Postmodernism's relativizing of false absolutes in every sphere has great potential for opening minds to**

new visions of truth. Its attention to diversity and to the marginal is turning our attention to the other in our midst and encouraging movements on every continent toward liberation of the oppressed.[34]

Schneiders is addressing the marginalizing of women while underlining that this is not a woman's issue but touches on all groups that are marginalized by the dominant culture. Although postmodernism tends to reject all master narratives, except the Market, it does seek a more inclusive agenda. It challenges western males to include the feminine as feminine (not as co-opted male) and in doing so to learn to accept the *other* as *different*. This brings us to the second aspect of Jesus' radical ministry: his willingness to work within Jewish boundaries and, at the same time his willingness to go beyond them.

Perhaps the most pressing sign of our times is the mass movement of people in our world. Millions are on the move today escaping war, persecution and poverty. Prosperous nations are confronted with this new phenomenon and are struggling to find an answer. Generally, it tends to be negative, reinforced by the fear of the foreigner and the stranger. The fear-filled perspective of the war on terror has hijacked western politics, which used to promote a utopian vision of hope and progress. When John Paul II invited the religious leaders of the world to Assisi, he opened up a very different vision. The most creative postmodern thinkers are promoting this open narrative. This is the place where religion and spirituality can begin to come together in a much more satisfying way.

For all its faults, religion has always tried to keep alive the memory of the poor and the marginalized. Spiritual seekers today are also reminding us of the need to recognise the mystery at the heart of the search for God. Dogmas, rituals and doctrines should help to build protective, but not watertight boundaries. The God of Jesus is more about inclusion than exclusion. Spirituality cannot be reduced to nice days by the side of lakes or on mountain peaks. If it is to retain vibrancy, it has to learn to embrace *the other*, especially when *the other* is poor, different, marginalized. In the twenty-first century, religious believers and spiritual seekers have to embrace the marriage of the feminine and the masculine, the mystical and the prophetic. We need people who are not afraid to sit in the belly of the whale, to lose control of the old agendas, and be ready to be spewed out onto a different shore. Deirdre Mullen, who works at the United Nations, spells out some implications for those who work in religious life:

---

34   Sandra M Schneiders *Beyond Patching* (Paulist Press Mahwah NJ 2004) p ix

This is a difficult time for religious congregations. The glory days are over and we live in a different era. The era of globalisation calls on religious to be fearless witnesses to the gospel. Our witness must be ecumenical rather than sectional. We must be people who give an overriding loyalty to humanity as a whole in order to preserve the best in our individual societies. This calls for a worldwide community that lifts neighbourly concern beyond one's tribe, race, class and nation.[35]

Religious orders have been founded in the Church to keep alive the tension between the institutional aspect of religion and its charismatic heart and soul. But in a secular age this challenge today is being addressed to all religious believers as we struggle to live harmoniously in what are being called *transcultural communities.*

The Church is facing new challenges, but matters of soul and spirit never change. The issue is always one of transformation, of moving from the ego-centred agenda of the false self to the deeper, wider reality of the true self, of moving from the small horizon of a parochial tribal view of God, to embrace and include the bigger picture. Here we come back to the issue of truth. Postmodernism always questions any attempt to put the whole truth into a package.

As Lieven Boeve states, Jesus is the very paradigm of the open narrative. In his contemplative way of viewing all reality, he reveals a God who is constantly interrupting and opening up all closed narratives that attempt to package God as exclusive, tribal, on our side:

Jesus offers those victims, who had been silenced by the closed narratives that dominated their context, the chance to speak up and invites them to participate in the open narrative that he himself proclaims and of which he himself is the example.[36]

This opening-up was to bring Jesus into direct conflict not just with the Pharisees and Scribes, who benefited from their closed interpretation of the

---

35 Deirdre Mullen, *Leadership: The Hard Questions*
(The Furrow, The Furrow Trust, Ireland 2004) p 600

36 Lieven Boeve *Interrupting Tradition* (Peters Press Louvain 2003) p 120

Jewish faith, but also with Herod and Pilate who sought to defend the closed political systems that kept the poor in subjection.

To move out of a closed system is to find another way of seeing. This demands moving beyond market-led consumer spirituality as lifestyle, to a much more courageous and challenging way of including the poor and the rejected, and giving them a voice. It means moving beyond charity, which keeps the poor in their place, to work for justice, which recognises the power of the oppressed, and being prepared to listen to *the truth of the Other.* This is much more challenging and perhaps explains why Jesus heals the blind man in Bethsaida in such a strange way. He takes him outside his local community. He rubs spittle on his eyes. Sometimes we need to move beyond the comfort of our familiar horizon and engage the pain and unpleasantness of trying to see *The Other.* At first, the man is still unable to see people, they look like trees to him. Jesus touches him again and then the man learns to see plainly and distinctly.

Fortunately, there are many courageous priests, lay pastoral workers, and teachers in schools trying to pass on the faith in these challenging times. Many work in areas of poverty and deprivation. They often describe the difficulty of helping to build an adult faith. The poor often lack the confidence to voice their concerns, to come to meetings, to play a part in building community. These pastoral leaders, often overstretched and overworked, are in a sense sitting in the belly of the whale, or trying to rub spittle into unwilling eyes. Their task should not be underestimated; but in many ways, they are the spiritual pathfinders and heroes of our time.

It has been suggested that the Church today is encountering a new Ephesian moment. This phrase has been coined by Andrew F. Walls.[37] It refers to that critical moment in the early Church at Ephesus when a Jewish and Gentile group came together as one community under the authority of Jesus. They understood, as did other communities in the early Church, the central nature of the reconciling mission of Jesus. This mission was to be inclusive and universal and expressed in the great transforming insight of Paul, the outsider who became an insider, the Jew who was also a Roman citizen:

> **There is no longer Jew or Greek, there is no longer slave or free, there is no longer male or female; for all of you are one in Christ Jesus.** *Galatians 3*

---

37 For more on the Ephesian Moment see *No Longer Strangers* (Dominican Publications Dublin 2006)

Today this challenge has been brought to the streets of our cities as we witness the arrival of many people of different cultures, religions and races. Now while postmodern thought seeks to include those from *below* or *the outsiders,* at the same time it has allowed the philosophy of the market to take centre stage. The whole point of the market is to include those who have money and exclude those who do not. While, *in theory,* postmodernism extends a welcoming hand to the poor and the rejected, *in practice*, it slams the door, rather firmly, in their faces.

In recent years, I have been working closely with asylum seekers. They receive minimal help from the state and they are not allowed to work. Some find ways of working illegally and are regularly exploited. A young asylum seeker told me the other day how he works for less than 50 pence an hour. Western countries have signed the 1951 UN Refugee Convention to accept anyone who seeks asylum on grounds of racial, religious or political persecution. In practice, it is clear that asylum seekers are not really wanted and governments are actively finding ways of *reducing the numbers.* When push comes to shove governments offer a welcome to anyone who can contribute to the economy, the great God of the Market, but without that membership ticket to the great Master Narrative of our times, asylum seekers are not welcome. Zygmunt Bauman puts it bluntly but accurately:

> **There are always too many of them. Them are the fellows of whom there should be fewer – or better still none at all. And there are never enough of us, Us are the folks of whom there should be more.**[38]

In his book *Wasted Lives,* Bauman makes the point that modern consumer societies live by the production of waste. Waste disposal is the underside of the endless array of ever-new products on the market. The great sin and shame today is to be out of date. Refugees and asylum seekers are the human face of this need to produce more and more waste. They are treated as human waste. It is interesting to see how most asylum seekers are located by governments in areas of social deprivation. It is not surprising there are tensions, which at times explode into acts of violence. Into this cocktail, the popular press adds its own poisonous ingredients by associating immigrants and asylum seekers with schemers and swindlers who border on the edge of criminality.

I have been suggesting that the great pattern of meaning we all have to discover and undergo is the Paschal Mystery. In order to enjoy the fullness of

---

38 Zygmunt Bauman *Wasted Lives* (Polity Press Cambridge 2004) p 34

life there has to be some kind of death experience, some dying to the small defensive world of the ego, the false self. At their best, all religions teach this and I have indicated that ancient cultures also intuited this with their initiation rites, especially for aggressive males. Sadly, in religious circles, you often meet people who show little evidence of such transformation. There are too many religious racists around, too many religious people who are rigid and unbending, showing few signs of compassion. I have also experienced some racism among asylum seekers, but rarely. More often than not, I meet people who have a great gentleness and serenity among them.

At the end of all human life is the great mystery of death. Even the rich, protected and surrounded by all their possessions, cannot escape this mystery. Spirituality and healthy religion suggest that we have to undergo some kind of death experience in order to live well. Postmodern society deals with death by denying it and placing healthy living at the top of the agenda. However, no matter what we do to stay healthy, we hear of people struck down by cancer, or by heart attacks; we hear of young children, even babies dying. Alternatively, we may experience death as some kind of failure in our lives. We lose our job, a relationship breaks down, or these things happen to people we know and love. We discover that we are not as *good* as we thought we were. This is the great crisis for good, church-going people. We try to do the right thing, we try to be loving and forgiving, and then we reach a point in life when we discover that we really are phoneys. Religious, spiritually aware people, discover that they are just as wounded as everybody else. This is the critical moment. What happens next is crucial. We can slip back into blaming somebody else, and we join the ranks of the bitter and cynical; or we can recognise that we ourselves cannot fix this problem, we cannot mend the wound and we cannot get out of the belly of the whale. We have to be spewed out by the circumstance of life. That is the moment of surrendering to the great mystery, what the Church calls the Paschal Mystery. We discover a God whose very purpose is to bring life out of death, to lead us into a new and true identity.

When I talk to asylum seekers, I often meet people who have known this death. A young man from Zimbabwe, escaping the horrors of the Mugabe regime, told me of how he slept rough on the streets of Manchester for a year. Another from Iran told me of how he spent days being transported across Europe in lorry after lorry, having no idea of where he was going. A married woman from Eastern Siberia told me how her husband's skull was fractured and she herself was raped. These people have undergone a kind of death before death, and they have come through it not with anger or bitterness but with wisdom and gentleness.

The foreigner, the immigrant, the asylum seeker, the handicapped person, the sick person, the poor person, all remind me of who I really am. That is what I need to see. I have to stop seeing people as *trees*[39] but as people, who are not a threat to my existence but who hold the key to my identity. The Spirit today is gently leading many searchers to a deeper awareness to recognise the presence of God in all things, in our planet, and in all people. This is the great mystical insight that reconciles the one and the many. Shortly before his death, Thomas Merton reminded us that we are already one, even though we think we are not, and what we have to become aware of is what we already are. It all comes down to identity.

Jesus became the great outsider, the cornerstone who was rejected by the political and religious leaders of his time. In his fundamentally contemplative attitude he revealed a God who, as both Father and Mother, loves us unconditionally and gives to all people a dignity and value far greater than anything that can be purchased or acquired. He invites us to move beyond our ego-centred lives to enter a world of mystery and grace in which all people are embraced and nothing is rejected. That is true seeing.

---

39   Matthew 20

Chapter 10 — Finding the Shape of our Souls

> Religion has to shift from moralism to mysticism, with less emphasis on the God out there and more emphasis on the God within. Perhaps in the past we did not need to relate personally and intensely to the God within, because the God without was already convincing, powerful, mighty and self-evident – this God focused our attention. But with the collapse in belief in the traditional image of God, we have to find God in a new place, and the most convincing place of all will be our own human hearts. This does not mean that God will be a merely personal experience, locked away in the closet of introspection, but rather the discovery of God in our interiority will be the basis for a new appreciation of God in the world. As Meister Eckhart wrote in the 14th century, *when God disappears from culture, we have to learn to give birth to God in the soul.*[40]

We live in two worlds. In the first half of life we centre most of our energy on the outer world, the world of career, achievement, getting married, building a home, bringing up children. In the second half of life a different agenda forces its way into our consciousness. It is the call of the inner journey. This is the hunger that comes from our souls, and it underlies so many of our current problems and discontents. Carl Jung once said that the key issue for every patient that came to him in the second half of life (over 35) was discovering a religious outlook on life. He said that they had all fallen ill because they had lost what all religions have tried to teach their followers. There is no doubt that we are experiencing a deep sense of loss today, loss of meaning, loss of direction, *a loss of soul*. I recently read a comment from Barack Obama, the rising star of the US Democratic Party, about a real sense that something is missing from many prosperous and successful people. At the same time, a British government minister is reporting on the crisis in families – across all social classes – caused by parents' dramatic loss of confidence in how to bring up their children. A culture that doesn't know how to pass on wisdom to its children is in deep trouble.

Today we need to discover the agenda for the second half of life. We need to find the shape of our souls. I think that the reason so many give up organised religion is because we are no longer feeding their soul hunger. We have given them morality, dogmas and doctrines – and they are needed as foundations

---

40 David Tacey *The Spirituality Revolution* (Brunner – Routledge UK 2004) p 193

– but we rarely take them beyond into the deep journey of the second half of life.

We don't help people to discover their deepest dream, what Jesus called *The Kingdom of God*. So we keep them at the agenda of the moral struggle, which only leads to anger and frustration at our continued failures. If I think of God primarily as a stern judge who is recording my every failure, then I am never going to fall in love with that kind of God. Jesus spent his whole ministry revealing to people the image of God that was already present in their souls. He told them to trust in that image and to let it grow. However, in order to do that they had to let go of all the false programmes for happiness, which the false self had built up in the first part of life: the need for power, possessions, reputation. He taught them to trust in a new and abundant life within them, the true self, the God-self, which was a free gift beyond all efforts to become worthy. He taught them that the God that they thought of as dwelling in heaven, beyond their reach, was so in love with them that he could be found in their very hearts and souls. He asked the question – the one Jung identified as the key to a meaningful life – *what does it matter if you amass a private fortune of great wealth, with all the energy that takes, if you suffer the loss of your own soul?* He chided his friend Martha, over worrying about so many things, while neglecting the one thing necessary.

Joseph Campbell spent his life studying the stories that people tell to express the connection between their outer and inner world. In his seminal book, *The Hero with a Thousand Faces*, he said that the inner journey is the greatest journey of the hero. This is the journey that connects all our essential relatedness: to ourselves, to family and friends, to others, and everything in the environment. We seem to have reached a stage in our culture when a new consciousness is trying to emerge. This is the Sacred Feminine, the eternal wisdom that is present in our God-created world. The masculine worldview with its stress on the outer world of achievement has to find a new balance with the feminine of the inner life. When feminism found its voice in the last century, it forced men to begin reflecting on the masculine dimensions of spirituality. Men as well as women came to see the need to reverse the great project of western culture: the replacement of the human soul with a consumer soul. Thinking people are feeling the inadequacy of this materialistic diet; we do not, as was famously said, *live by bread alone.*

Our culture will not give up without a fight. One of its great distractions today is the cult of celebrity. The media live off the lives of celebrities, and feed every bit of news and gossip into our souls. This is not an attack on the individuals involved, but the cumulative effect is to shift our inner lives onto the outer lives of the celebrities. It takes away our own greatness of soul as our humdrum lives are constantly compared with the rich and famous and their competing egos. It is interesting to note the response of Jesus when people wanted to make him king: he walked away. When someone praised his goodness, he said, *Why do you do that,* and he pointed to the goodness of his Father. When he encountered the rich, he challenged them; when he met the poor and rejected, he told them about their dignity as sons and daughters of God.

Can we describe the shape of our souls? Jung and Campbell would argue that what makes us great is buried deep within us. Jung spoke of *archetypes*, sources of energy and power that lie deep in what he called the collective unconscious. These archetypes are found in all cultures, in literature, and in dreams. Some have identified the archetypes as masculine, but I would agree with Bruce Tallman who claims that they are, in fact, universal and can be found in the male and the female psyche.

All human beings have masculine and feminine characteristics within them, and when people are fully mature they have integrated the masculine and feminine into their personalities. For example, the fully mature male knows how to be compassionate, intuitive and receptive as well as strong, and the fully mature female knows how to be assertive, direct and decisive as well as loving.[41]

The Bible begins with a ringing declaration that we are all, male and female, made in the image and likeness of God. There is a rich variety of archetypes, but they can be seen as sub groups of four major ones, which can be described as *The Sovereign, The Warrior, The Seer, and The Lover.* Each type has positive and negative features. We are conflicted beings, we never get it all together, but we know in which direction maturity lies. The spiritual journey is never a simple linear progression, as our ordered minds might prefer. It is always learning to live with some steps forward and some steps backward. Earlier in the book, I said that Christ is present in our hearts and souls in a cruciform way. Learning to carry that mystery is the key to spiritual transformation rather than ten steps to a mature and happy life. Psychology can only take us so far, as Jung pointed out. We will always limp like Jacob; we are a mixture of the heroic and the anti-heroic.

---

41 Bruce Tallman *Archetypes for Spiritual Direction* (Paulist Press NJ 2005) p 15

1. Sovereign, King, Queen, Leader[42]

In a sense, the other three archetypes all flow from this one, which expresses the need for order and security: without it we have chaos and disorder. Our postmodern culture is still uneasy about authority as we react to some of the abuses and excesses of past oppressive regimes, both political and religious. We all need a certain degree of safety and security, in which a culture or community, or a family can flourish. The wise sovereign or leader creates an atmosphere of peace and calm allowing everyone to develop his or her different gifts for the benefit of all; providing the necessary laws and boundaries for the protection of all, preventing the weak being exploited by the strong. The Bible begins with a strong emphasis on structures and good laws. We see how fundamental the Ten Commandments, given by God to Moses, became to the life and memory of the chosen people. Jesus takes this further and radicalises all law in the eight beatitudes with their subversion of any power structure that diminishes the poor and the weak.

A good sovereign is also the guarantee of the creative energy in a culture or community. As the Grail legend points out, if the ruler is sick the whole realm shares the sickness. A vital gift of any leader is the gift of blessing. All of us have a deep need for approval, not in the egocentric way of the false self, but at a deep level of soul. A friend of mine in the USA sent me an article from the Wall Street Journal written at the time of the recent papal election. The journalist described how office workers stopped what they were doing and ran to St Peter's Square. They craned their necks in the large crowd, to receive a blessing from the man in white, the newly-elected pope. This kind of blessing reminds us that we do not have to construct our true identity. It is part of the sacred world of mystery, to which we are always connected. This is not just a prerogative of ordained ministers. All the baptised share to some degree in the priesthood of Christ, and fathers, mothers, teachers all have this gift to bless those in their care with words and gestures of affirmation. Today there is a crying need for this archetype. In families, we need good mothers and good fathers who can provide calm, clear and loving guidance to the young.

When parents try to care for the economic well being of their families, putting bread on the table, they are acting as sovereigns. When teachers strive to create an orderly environment in which the young can grow and develop, they are energised by the sovereign archetype. The same applies to leaders of

---

42 For a fuller discussion see Robert Moore and Douglas Gillette , *King, Warrior, Magician, Lover* (Harper Collins San Francisco 1990) Carol Pearson, *Awakening the Heroes Within* (Harper San Francisco 1991) Tad and Noreen Guzie, *About Men and Women*, (Paulist Press NY 1986)

companies, or union leaders, when they work with integrity and respect rather than by exploiting their members. The sovereign archetype also knows that we are not just put on this Earth to work. Play, too, is important, as is rest and relaxation. (The workaholic has lost the bigger picture.) They recognise their own limits and of those in their care. They rule not from their false and needy selves, but the true self. They are centred and serene. They have authority without being authoritarian.

Perhaps one of the gifts of authentic monotheistic religion to our fragmented postmodern world is to remind us that God holds everything together. This includes all aspects of our lives, the good – and this is the great teaching – and also the bad, the light and the dark, the wheat and the weeds. A good leader will know how to reassure when times are dark, because a good leader can see in the dark. Mature leaders have to exhibit all the other archetypes. As good warriors, they will protect those in their care. As seers they will grasp the bigger picture and, equally important, know how to communicate it. This is one of the most demanding responsibilities for leaders in our postmodern world, but it is needed more than ever.

The negative or shadow-side of the sovereign is the weak leader or the tyrant. The tyrant is the dictator, the overbearing boss, the too strict parent, the rigid leader who will never compromise, the pastor who cannot get beyond the letter of the law. We have seen plenty of examples of ruthless dictators in recent history: Hitler, Stalin, Pol Pot, Saddam Hussein, Robert Mugabe. In Liberia I witnessed the suffering and devastation caused by the tyrannical rule of Charles Taylor. They are obsessed with power and its trappings. They seek total control over the lives of others. Their god is their ego. The tyrannical male is the man who uses violence against his wife or his children. The tyrannical ruler or leader is often threatened by the emergence of the new. In the manner of King Herod, the tyrant is always threatened by new life. He is destructive rather than creative. A healthy leader is not threatened in this way and is happy to promote younger people and give them responsibility.

To access this archetype it is necessary to let go of the ego and recognise that the gift of leadership is not a personal possession, but a service to be rendered. Jesus reminds his egocentric disciples of this hard truth:

> **You know that among the Gentiles those whom they recognise as their rulers lord it over them, and their great ones are tyrants over them. But it shall not be so among you; whoever wishes to become great among you must be your servant, and whoever wishes to become first among you must be slave to all.** *Mark.10*

Jesus was very conscious of how easy it is to be seduced by power. Sadly we have seen this in the Church in recent times. All of us have something of this power within us and too often the laity have abdicated their own power to the clergy and too many clergy abrogate all the power to themselves. This does not lead to a healthy state of affairs, and contradicts the mature use of power modelled by Jesus.

2. Warrior

We all have the energy of a good warrior within us. This energy is what drives us to accomplish a good cause. It provides the spirit and resilience to overcome problems and to respond to challenges. It fuels the artist and the poet to working creatively, even in hard times. It drives a mother to protect and care for her children. It can be seen in all those heroic men and women who work for peace and justice in all parts of the world, those who dedicate their lives and energy to help others.

An obvious example of warrior energy is the soldier. Where historically that was the preserve of the male, now women also can serve in the military. Nevertheless, the warrior archetype is the primary energy source for the male. Opinion polls often show a drop in respect for leaders today, but soldiers are held in high regard. We all admire courage, bravery and self-sacrifice. Nevertheless, warriors need good leadership, good sovereigns, and sadly, in recent times, we have seen soldiers abusing their power over prisoners and civilians. Historically there were important codes of chivalry for warriors to prevent abuses of violence. In the technological sophisticated warfare of today that is becoming more difficult.

Some women in the feminist movement have attacked male warrior energy, nevertheless it is a vital part of what drives people to achieve and build a better world. Warriors need to serve, rather than enjoy total control. Most advanced nations have separated military from political leadership. When the military take control of a country the leadership often becomes toxic and dictatorial. A good warrior knows when to use force and when not to, when to speak the truth and when to keep silent. They can access the energy of the seer in this respect as well as the lover when they are mature enough to act with compassion.

Good warriors have to know when to act and how to act decisively in the face of problems. They are good planners and work out appropriate strategies and tactics. Planning has long been associated with the world of warfare and business. Today it is increasingly being found in the Church and in religious congregations, as they struggle to shape the future in a rapidly changing world, and not be deflected by those who are afraid of change. This is good warrior energy and is a key element in leadership today. Since we face so many problems the temptation is to shrink from all action and just let things drift.

In religious history, we see the warrior archetype in the figure of the prophet. Jesus often adopted the language and style of the prophets as he defended the poor and the weak against all forms of oppression. He defined his whole ministry in terms of bringing good news to the poor. As the Jewish prophets courageously denounced the injustices of the Jewish monarchy, Jesus confronted the religious and political oppression of his day, which led to his death. He took this confrontation with evil and injustice to a whole new level in his complete rejection of violence. Only today are we beginning to understand how central non-violence was to the mission of Jesus. He preached forgiveness and even love of enemies. He even preached forgiveness from the very cross on which he was nailed. At times, we have reduced Jesus to a rather anaemic and weak figure: gentle Jesus, meek and mild. In fact, he showed amazing courage and love for life. He wasn't afraid to present God's love as demanding and conditional at times, which is a very masculine way of loving.

The initiation ceremonies of ancient cultures knew the danger of uncontrolled aggression, which is a very male problem, as we see today in gang culture and destructive violence. That is why they led young males through some kind of ritual humiliation, some scarring and some wounding, that they hoped would lead to the development of mature warrior energy. The dark warrior is always a danger especially in a society like today that has so few clear boundaries. When it is *every man for himself*, then the strong will always bully the weak. In the untransformed life, the dark warrior will appear not just on our streets but in our boardrooms, or our classrooms, even our parishes and religious communities.

The same can be true of those working for peace and justice. If action for justice is rooted in anger, rather than compassion and love, then it will not build the Kingdom. Healthy warriors must face and own their own anger. That is why Jesus warned about taking the splinter from our brother's eye while neglecting the plank in our own.

3. Seer, Wise Man, Wise Woman, Magician (Magi)

This is the most difficult archetype for our western society to understand. Our left-brain, logical and scientific culture has great difficulty with the Wisdom figure, the Seer. The founders of all the great religions of the world were

Seers. Ancient cultures had their magi or magicians, priests, shamans, witch doctors, astrologers, soothsayers who could do amazing things. They were credited with great insight and wisdom, and were often employed in the role of court advisors. The seer is gifted with a different level of consciousness, an awareness of the need for transformation. The Seer is the wise man or woman who can guide a society and community towards positive rather than negative transformation. It is interesting to see that the leaders of the recently revived men's movements are totally open to the importance of the feminine in seeking true and authentic wisdom for our times. This coming together of the masculine and the feminine can be described as the very centre of the spirituality revolution in our times, the marriage of the inner and the outer world. Institutional religion that resists this development will continue to lose its grip on people's lives.

Seers lead us back to rediscover our souls. They help us to re-align our lives with what is true and real. This is what Jesus meant when he stressed the importance of being grafted onto the vine. Where the warrior moves to action, the Seer is energised by thinking, by insight, by reflection, and by contemplation. They are the ones who can see the bigger picture. They have a sense that everything is related, that everything belongs. They know how to weep at the tragedy of life and also celebrate its joys. They have a feel for the paradox and complexity at the heart of human experience. So much of the teaching of Jesus was wisdom teaching: using parables and stories rather than doctrinal instruction.

Our postmodern world seems to prefer cheap answers to wisdom. Twenty-four hour media demand instant answers from politicians and leaders to every problem. No one is permitted to say, *I don't know.* The ego seems to prefer answers rather than learning to see in the dark. We prefer outer authority to inner authority. Even the magi in the Christmas story were changed into three kings without any scriptural evidence.

There has to be some semblance of spirituality for a wise man or wise woman to emerge. There has to be some willingness to go beyond analytical thinking. The spiritual disciplines of prayer and contemplation can take the wise person beyond the everyday mindset to a deeper more mystical awareness. This is not to replace thinking, but to marry it with the more non-rational realm of wisdom. In this age of information overload there is a real need for wisdom as well as cleverness. We need people who can see in the dark. To do this the Seer must make the inner journey. The Seer has to have let go of the egocentric agenda and learned to surrender to the Great Mystery. This is crucial, as Jesus says: *Physician, heal yourself.*

The shadow of this archetype is the manipulator or the trickster. Manipulators don't allow people to grow up. They want to keep them at an immature level. We see this in businesses that do not want anyone to rock the boat by asking awkward question. Party politics has become highly organised. Members have to be *on message*. No one can deviate from the party line. Sadly, the Church also has often promoted company men, compliant bishops and clergy. Here again power is being abused. Jesus had very strong words for those who wanted to wear long flowing robes and be greeted obsequiously in the market place. True Seers know that they are nothing in the great scheme of things, other than the power bestowed on them from on high. They can laugh at their weaknesses and don't take themselves too seriously.

4. The Lover

The lover is the one who makes the deepest connections about life. The lover embraces life with great passion, enthusiasm, and joy. At the same time, the lover is able to embrace the pain of suffering and be transformed by it rather than become embittered. Jesus is the great lover archetype revealing what we most needed to hear and see: that God is love, compassion, mercy, forgiveness, joy unconfined, extravagance, exuberance. He has this amazing ability to relate to everyone, especially those who felt burdened by suffering. He is happy on his own in prayer to his Father; he is happy with his disciples and with crowds. He clearly enjoyed sitting down at table to enjoy food and wine, and unashamedly defended this before his critics:

> **To what shall I compare this generation? It is like children sitting in the market places and calling out to one another, we played the flute for you, and you did not dance; we wailed and you did not mourn.** *Matthew 11*

He is telling them to grow up. He shows great tenderness to all, and on the Cross demonstrates the greatest lesson ever taught on non-violence. As a mature lover, he was at home in his body, and in a heavily patriarchal culture he welcomed, embraced, and enjoyed the friendship of women.

The mature lover has a sense of the underlying unity of all things in a world of great diversity. This is the vision of the mystic. Lovers integrate all the archetypes. They honour the boundaries of the sovereign that must characterise all relationships, but are prepared to go beyond them in the name of love. They manifest the drive and passion of the warrior and are prepared to give their lives for others, especially the poor. They can also show the tough love that is demanded at certain times. They exhibit the wisdom of the Seer and taste the contemplative vision that sees God in all things.

Although the mature lover is the most attractive human archetype it has not been easy to live at this level of maturity. Both religion and secular culture have struggled to get it right. Religion has often appeared threatened by the lover. Despite the beauty of the Incarnation, of God taking flesh in Jesus, religion has not felt comfortable with the whole area of human sexuality. We have tended to err on the side of the negative. This is the negative shadow of the lover, described as Frigid or Impotent. It describes men and women who are out of touch with their own warmth and feelings. They are not the easiest people to live with; they radiate anxiety about life. They are not communicators of joy. They are often depressed and, frankly, depressing to be with.

Secular culture, on the other hand, has gone down the road of rejecting all boundaries in pursuit of endless sexual pleasure. The only advice given to the young is *practise safe sex*. This often-trotted-out phrase reflects little awareness of the damage that trivialised sex does to the soul. This is the shadow addictive lover. Without limits and boundaries, we are at the mercy of our most selfish instincts. Once a relationship becomes difficult, the addict moves on to the next one. They know how to take, but not how to give, as they strive to fill the hunger and ache in their souls. They have failed to heed the warning of the ancient commandment: to have no false gods. Their only god is their ego.

At the end of our searching what do we find? I think we find that the beauty and grandeur of our souls is a flawed beauty and grandeur. This may be a disappointment to many. Modernity rejected religion and tried to build a secular utopia based on reason. Universal education, science and technology would deliver widespread prosperity and happiness for all. After its failures in the terrible world wars of the twentieth century, postmoderns retreated into a cocoon of cynicism and anger, rejecting all great patterns of meaning. If religion simply plays the moral card, we are all condemned to endless failures. Where is the good news in that? Nor can human life be reduced to the private bliss agenda of some spiritualities. All we can do is to carry the mystery of who we are. That is all God wants from us. What we crucify, God can raise up. Where we hate, God brings love. When we fail, God offers forgiveness. All souls are a mixture of the heroic and the anti-heroic. All that matters is that we learn the mystery of love and compassion, for others, for our enemies, and perhaps, most difficult of all, for ourselves.

Holbein's painting *Noli Me Tangere* reminds us that we do not sit in the brilliant light of the angels. We stand in the early light of dawn with Mary Magdalene gazing in wonder at the Risen Christ who shares the dawn light with us. He holds up his wounded hands and calls her by name. Looking at the wounded and glorified body the seeker has been found. If she is to experience the fullness of this new risen life, she has to be prepared to let go of old ways of knowing, to move from the false egocentric self into the life of the true God-self. As the angel asks: *Why look for the living among the dead?*

Lord of creativity, stay with us when we are lost and waiting.

Give us time to let the deadness of the past slip away from us,

and help us to see the way ahead to new patterns and possibilities.

May the path of your Resurrection continue to unfold in these times.

Help us to be aware of your Spirit

nudging us and annoying us into action.

May we play our part in bringing the light of Resurrection

into the sometimes confusing pattern

of plans and relationships in our world.[43]

---

43 D O'Malley Via Lucis (Don Bosco Publications)

Other Books by Michael Cunningham

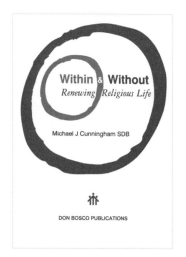

Within & Without

Don Bosco Publications 2003

God is present in all aspects of our human experience, good and bad. By accepting ourselves, and learning to love others, we are drawn into a love of the enchanted yet flawed world in which we live. Though this book is primarily for Religious, it will help all of us make sense of the challenges facing us today.

A Time for Compassion

Don Bosco Publications 2005

As Christian believers, our lives only make sense when we can unite our personal and group stories with what God is doing for the whole of humanity. In the Gospel, we see Jesus creating groups of friends whose love is secure enough to widen the circle of human acceptance and love in a spirituality of compassion and forgiveness for all people.

Credits